```
   .11 011'
   .1010 100(
  J101010 111(
  01011111 001        M000189840
 1 01000011 00011100 11100010 10011100 011
 .0 10110101 10011001 11001011 01001001 111(
 10 10010010 10000010 00100011 00011111 000(
 1 10000000 01100110 10111001 01010010 0110
 '1 01100111 00000101 00100011 11010010 100'
 '00110111 00100001 01000101 01010001 00'
  '1111101 11011001 11001010 11101000 1'
   '11111 11010011 10001100 1000110'
   '011 11000101 10001011 01000('
     ' 01001111 10100101 0'
        (011 1(
        .1101 '
        .101'
        .1(
```

SPEAKING THEIR LANGUAGE

The Non-Techie's Guide to Managing IT & Cybersecurity for Your Organization

ROB PROTZMAN

Cover image by: Alex_82, 99 Designs
Book design by: SWATT Books Ltd

Printed in the United States
First Printing, 2021

ISBN: 978-1-7376739-0-3 (Paperback)
ISBN: 978-1-7376739-1-0 (eBook)

Standard 3.1 Publishing
Loveland, Colorado
80537

www.s3p1.com

CONTENTS

FOREWORD

In 2017, I found myself the proud and intimidated new CEO for a small/medium-sized nonprofit organization, Boys & Girls Clubs of Larimer County. For me, this was the dream job, the one that I had been training for since the start of my work with the organization, eight years prior. I learned quickly that my "training" wasn't as detailed as I would have hoped. In fact, it lacked a couple of key points that had the potential to severely disrupt our ability to function if I didn't figure out how to manage them properly. That is when I really got to know Rob Protzman and his team at Chartered Technology.

On several occasions within my first six months, I found myself in deep conversations with Rob as he would walk me through options to increase our cybersecurity, upgrade infrastructure and maximize our ability to work with kids through technology. Rob would explain the pros and cons of different platforms, discuss price considerations, and would even help me strategize how to fund these projects. As time went on, I realized that these conversations were rather abnormal, in that my colleagues were not having the same level of conversations with their IT companies. Some of my fellow nonprofit leaders were still distributing used and recycled devices from the late 90s while constantly battling internet outages/outdated financial management systems/ hacking attempts and more. They did this all while paying the same if not more than we were for IT service, if they had IT service at all. Many nonprofit leaders are conditioned to believe that they are supposed to get by on the bare minimum, that high functioning technology and IT systems are a luxury only to be used by successful for-profit organizations.

I am so thankful that is not our reality when it comes to IT management. With Rob and his team, we get to live from a place of plenty, not scarcity. To be clear, that does not mean we always have the dollars to spend - it meant that we have a partner to help us make smart financial decisions. I attribute this to Rob. First, that is just the type of person he is, and second, that is the type of culture and company he has built. Rob partners with his clients, he knows the struggles of nonprofits and small businesses, he has lived in both of those worlds. He is passionate about helping people succeed, whether that means late phone calls, weekend work, fundraising assistance, funding assistance (in our case) or sometimes a Friday evening meeting over a beer - Rob is there.

There have been so many lessons I have learned since 2017 and the most important one for me is: surround yourself with good people. Rob and Chartered Technology are without a doubt the kind of good people you want to surround yourself with. They will make IT management manageable by helping you strategize, alleviate weak spots and stay up to date in this fast-paced environment. Most importantly, they will look out for your success, they will think about your business as if it were their own. While technology is certainly not my forte, it is something that has not hindered our organization's success and that is because of who we partner with. I would highly recommend other organizations and/or new CEOs to consider if they can say the same.

Kaycee Headrick, CEO
Boys & Girls Clubs of Larimer County

INTRODUCTION

I have heard it said a thousand times, "Where there's mystery, there's margin." It has always driven me a little nuts. On one hand, who is running a business that does not want to get more margin? On the other hand, it feels sleazy to me. If I am only paying a premium for something because I do not understand it, then I am probably getting ripped off. Do not get me wrong. There are a lot of things I do not understand and am happy to pay for. But, if I am paying a premium for something, there better be a lot of value that is being added - not just a few extra *margin points* due to my lack of knowledge.

I have written this book to take the mystery out of managing Information Technology (IT). Stick with me! I promise this is not a technical manual. I will start with who this book is not for: **this book is not for system administrators or technical support personnel**. It does not go into technical detail on how to run IT systems. There are plenty of great resources for that - this is not one of them. **This book is for business owners, upper management, non-profit directors, and anyone who wants to make sure their technology is being managed properly**, whether it is being handled by an internal employee or an outsourced service provider. While I did not write this book to be a how-to for our competitors, I hope they read it and implement it. If they do, their clients will be better off, which is good for everyone in the long run.

My expertise on this topic does not come from a book or a college curriculum. I am far from the poster child for your traditional IT management expert. In fact, most people laugh when I tell them my educational background. I do not believe they think it in itself is funny, but more so that, with my background, I run an IT company. Back in college, I tried just about every major which Colorado State University had to offer - okay, not that many, but quite a few. My father was an electrical engineer, and I really wanted to be like him, so that is what I started out with. By *started out with*, I mean I wrote it down and told my school counselor. After a very brief conversation, I learned that I should have thought about that a lot sooner. It sounded cool, but I had not actually done any preparation for such a degree, and so finishing college in 4 years wasn't a likely scenario if I went that route - for good reason, that major was off the table.

I worked my way through the general education requirements and took a few classes that seemed interesting. I loved computers, so I took some computer programming classes, figuring I would love that too. I did not. The only 'F' I have on my college transcript is from a four-credit Java programming course. To this day I cannot comprehend how people enjoy writing computer code. In the summer between my sophomore and junior year, I took a course called Human Development and Family Studies (HDFS). The pendulum had swung far from engineering - HDFS graduates typically end up with jobs in various social services. I really liked it, and I will be honest, it did not hurt that I was one of only three guys in the whole class. I decided to dig deeper into HDFS and soon needed to select where to do my practicum. I ended up at the Fort Collins Boys & Girls Club and was instantly drawn to the tech lab. I learned that I could help kids in need through teaching them about technology, and I never turned back.

I promise this book is about how to ensure your organization has properly managed IT and not my career trajectory, so I will *yadayada* the next part and skip ahead. During college I worked for a youth ministry in various capacities. One of those was helping them with their computers. It provided me the opportunity to gain a relatively good foundation for IT support, and after college, I went to work for the Boys & Girls Clubs of Larimer County as their IT Director. I was helping club members learn about technology while supporting the computers, networks, and servers for the organization. It was a golden opportunity. While I may have been the IT director, I was still pretty green, and they had an IT company contracted to do the 'real work' and make sure things were actually running properly. I watched the IT company closely, and I found their focus was strictly on the technical side of things. They did not expend much if any of their energy on ensuring that the people who relied on the tech had what they needed. It was all about the update or the maintenance. It just did not make sense to me. How could you support systems so that an organization could operate, without having a deep connection with the people and the organization itself? I learned some incredibly valuable lessons about the IT industry and, most importantly, the things it was lacking.

While working in the nonprofit world was incredibly rewarding, it did not provide the financial resources I needed to start a family. So, in 2009, I decided to create the kind of IT company that I wish existed. I started Protzman Technology Solutions, LLC. It was not exactly the most creative name. After mocking up a quick logo design and sending it to my buddy, Ryan, he pointed out that my logo actually read as 'Protz Tech Man Solutions.' I quickly changed the name to Chartered Technology, because I was not in the business of providing "man solutions" (whatever that means). Regardless of the name, I was determined to make sure technology worked so that people could use it to do amazing things like serve children in our community.

My first client was the Boys & Girls Clubs. They stuck with me through the transition, and for that I am eternally grateful. I will never forget the initial meeting with my second client, New Vision Charter School. I wanted to take over the management of their IT. Their board member, Daryl, who was tasked with vetting me, said something along the lines of, "Let us see how things go" when I told him I would need full administrative access to all of the systems. He made it clear that I would be there to provide technical support for teachers, and I had not quite earned my way into being the head honcho of IT quite yet. It did not take too long to gain their confidence and before long I was in 100% control of their technology.

As I grew Chartered Technology, one thing never changed: my mission to make technology work so that people can use it to be successful. This mission is why I started the business and is still what guides us today. In the early 2000s, our focus was mostly about keeping technology running - today our responsibilities have become far more complex due to advanced cybersecurity threats. While building the business, I spent an enormous amount of time trying to keep up with the constantly changing world of technology. It was my responsibility to make sure my clients had what they needed, and I took that part of the job very seriously. But as time went on, I became more obsessed with the non-technical side of IT service.

There was so much more to IT than all the technical information I had learned. As I dug in, determined to find a better way to manage IT, I came across Gary Pica. He talked extensively about the non-technical side of managing IT, and I was hooked. I have never met Gary, but I have watched countless hours of his videos and even went through his training course on running an IT company. As far as I know, he coined the term vCIO - virtual Chief Information Officer, which I will use in this book. The idea Gary posed was that small- to medium-sized businesses did not have someone looking out for them the way larger businesses did with their CIO, but just because these businesses did not have a CIO didn't mean they lacked the need for one. There is so much more to maintaining an organization's technology than keeping that *thing* running or fixing that annoying issue. I was determined to build my business in a way that provided this much-needed service. When my company took a step back and started providing our clients with IT services the way an internal CIO would, we had value. REAL value. Hiding in a closet and coming out looking like a magician when everything was fixed was good and all, but integrating ourselves into the organizations we worked with so that we could help them understand the bigger picture and achieve their goals provided a significantly better result for everyone involved.

Too many organizations think that they only need IT support and are unaware of the other critical components that they need to have in place. IT support is without a doubt a critical part of managing IT properly, but it is only one piece of a sustainable Information Technology solution. I want you to have the other pieces. I want you to know more about the technology you rely on. With a deeper understanding, you will be able to better manage your internal or outsourced IT services. You will be able to better guide your organization towards a future that is both reliable and sustainable. The good news is that most of this is not technical in nature. Sure, you will need technical people to properly implement and support these solutions, but the ideas are simple. The things you can keep an eye on to ensure your organization is set up for success are simple, and ones you are fully capable of understanding. In this book, I will guide you through the things you need to ensure are in place for your organization and provide you the tools needed in your position to make sure they are implemented properly. Let's get started.

Chapter 1:

THE RISKS ARE REAL

I often joke, "Our company is switching entirely to tablets - break out the stone and chisel, we are going old-school." In the '90s and early 2000s, a lot of things were done using computers, simply because they could be. It was new and exciting. Do not get me wrong, there were plenty of things that were truly enhanced with computers, but that is not always the case. I continue to see computers and technology being used as a solution in search of a problem, and I think there is merit in determining if a non-technical method works best before throwing a bunch of time and money into a computer-based solution. One example of this is note-taking. I keep a note-taking journal on my desk. It sits just in front of my keyboard, surrounded by 3 large computer monitors. There are several things in my office that are there for novelty's sake, but this is not one of them. I find that writing notes by hand allows me to remember the information better. It turns out there is science to back this up. The details of this have been studied and were published in *Psychological Science*[1] by Pam A. Mueller of Princeton University and Daniel M. Oppenheimer of the University of California, Los Angeles. There are TONS of note-taking apps, though. Microsoft has *OneNote*, Apple has *Notes*, Google has *Keep* and Evernote remains one of the most popular options. I do agree these have their place, but it is very common that the problem these apps 'fix' either does not exist or it does not actually fix it. Users battle these apps in meetings and in classrooms in an attempt to force a computer-based solution where it isn't actually needed. As we look around our offices and review the technical solutions we have in place, a lot of them do have merit, and have become an essential component of the way we function. Without a doubt, we can do more and do it better thanks to modern technology.

With these great rewards come great risks, and proper management of these technologies is key. Technical risks present themselves in three main avenues: 1) Mistakes 2) Security 3) System failures. It is important to understand what these risks are and how they impact our organizations. With a better understanding of these risks, we have a better understanding of what we need to do to reduce them. I want to ensure you understand that last sentence. Our objective is to reduce risks. While the idea of eliminating risks is attractive, it is not often feasible. At a certain point the costs, both in actual money spent and in lost revenue/productivity, become larger than the risk itself. The need to find a healthy balance between cost and risk will be a moving target, and I have provided you tools to assist with this in later chapters.

One of the most common misconceptions among small- to medium-sized businesses and nonprofits is that they are at a lower risk of technical and security related problems than larger organizations, and that those problems are not as severe when they do occur. While that may have been the case very early on, it simply is not true now. Our organizations rely so heavily on technology for even our most basic operations. When technical systems are not functioning properly, we cannot produce products or deliver services. When we lose data, we must recreate it. When information falls into the wrong hands, our reputations suffer. When any of these go badly wrong, we must close our doors. I invite you to take a moment and reflect on the impact these types of problems would have on your organization. Here are some uncomfortable questions worth posing:

» How long can you afford for your systems to be down?
» How long can you afford to pay your employees while you are not bringing any money in the door?
» How much would it cost to recreate or redesign the data you have stored digitally?
» How receptive would your clients be to finding out their information was stolen by cyber criminals?

When you begin to imagine these things, you begin to understand how important it is to protect against these risks. They are real, but there are ways to protect against them.

MISTAKES

Like many things, computers work well until we, people, start to use them. Unlike computers that work in simple binary - yes or no - terms, we are complex. Our complexity can lead to mistakes, and mistakes can lead to major problems for our organizations. Mistakes come in two forms, user error and bad security hygiene.

User errors occur when people do something with good intentions that causes problems. Oftentimes we see this in terms of people deleting files they believe are no longer needed, or modifying data to meet their needs, which ends up causing a problem for someone else. Sometimes user errors go beyond a missing file or modified data. On February 28, 2017, a huge chunk of the internet stopped working. Parts of websites would load, but things like images would not show up. Services like Airbnb and Slack experienced disruptions. Down Detector, a website and service that allows users to report issues with popular technical services, was itself down. Thoughts of a terrible cyber-attack or major nation state espionage were going through my head that day. How could so much of the internet be down all at the same time? It turns out, someone made a mistake. It is hard to argue the mistake they made was even that big of a mistake, but it had huge consequences. While performing maintenance, a technician at Amazon Web Services (AWS) typed a command into a computer. The command had a typo. It was intended to make some changes to a small group of their servers, but it ended up making changes to a very large group of servers. One set of servers that was impacted controlled the ability for the AWS's Simple Storage Solution (S3) to make files available. When these files became unavailable, any website that relied on AWS[2] S3 to host their files became crippled. Accidental file deletions, typos in maintenance commands, changing the wording in a shared document. All easy mistakes to make, none caused by malicious intent. Unfortunately, these mistakes cause down-time or lost productivity while the error is fixed, or the information is recreated. While a user error at your organization might not have the level of impact on the world that AWS's outage had, it can have a major impact on your ability to function.

Bad security hygiene is a nice way of saying that your employee's cybersecurity skills stink. The problems that come from users making cybersecurity mistakes can be catastrophic. In 2019 Kaspersky Lab[3] reported that 90% of data breaches in the cloud happened because employees fell for a social engineering attack. A social engineering attack is when a bad actor, like a cybercriminal, tricks someone into providing information or access to information that they should not be allowed to have. Kevin Mitnick's *Ghost in the Wires* is a highly insightful and educational read on this topic. In it, he details his "adventures as the world's most wanted hacker". His go-to method for gaining unauthorized access to systems was social engineering, and it worked incredibly well for him. It continues to be one of the most effective and popular hacking methods today. We will dig deeper into this as we explore security risks in Chapters 7 and 8, but even though this is a 'security related' risk, it is a result of humans making mistakes. Mistakes that continue to cause mass chaos for organizations around the world.

SECURITY

We see the results of security risks to organizations in the headlines daily. As I write this, we are still learning the details about one of the largest security breaches in history, the SolarWinds hack. It is believed that the US department of Homeland Security, State, Commerce and Treasury Departments, as well as the National Institute of Health, were all breached in this attack. Along with these government agencies, several private sector businesses were breached, including Microsoft, Intel, Cisco and cybersecurity firm FireEye. In early January 2021, the Federal Bureau of Investigation (FBI), the Cybersecurity and Infrastructure Security Agency (CISA) the Office of the Director of National Intelligence (ODNI), and the National Security Agency (NSA), released a joint statement[4] indicating Russia was to blame for the attacks. While you may be relatively confident that you are not on the radar of a foreign government, every time a breach like this occurs, tools and knowledge become available to other cybercriminals, who are just looking to make a buck.

When I look at security risks to small- and medium-size organizations, I break them into two categories: insider threats and external threats. While it is easy for us with small organizations to brush over the idea of an insider threat and assume the only real threats we face are external, I assure you insider threats are worth paying attention to.

Insider Threats
Insider threats come in two flavors, pawns and turncloaks. Security incidents due to insider threats are not always the result of a malicious employee. As discussed earlier, one of the most common methods used to breach organizations is a social engineering attack. This is when a pawn is used to carry out an attack. Phishing is one of the most common methods. Phishing is the fraudulent practice of sending emails to individuals that appear to be legitimate but

are actually sent by a cybercriminal with the intent of tricking the individual, or pawn, into providing sensitive data such as passwords or credit card numbers. In January 2020, a school district in Texas lost $2.3 million due to a phishing scam. Oftentimes we see what are called spear phishing emails. These are highly targeted emails created by cyber criminals, AKA bad actors, who have done their research. This last year, one of the most common ones we saw amongst our clients was related to gift cards. I am proud to say that none of our clients fell for these, and I attribute that to their good security hygiene.

Here are how these attacks work. The bad actor spends a few minutes browsing a company's website. We will call this fictional company Jumbo Products. On the Jumbo Products' website, they find a page listing the employees and learn the name and email addresses of the business owner, whom we will call John, and the front desk person whom we will call Mike. The bad actor goes to a free email service and creates an email address using the owner John's name. They send an email to Mike, the front desk person, and the conversation goes something like this:

```
To: Mike@jumboproducts.com
From: John-Jumbo@gmail.com
Subject: Mike - I need your help

Mike, do you have a moment? I have a request I
need you to handle discreetly. I am going into a
meeting now and can't take a call, so just reply
to my email.

John

----------
```

To: John-jumbo@gmail.com
From: mike@jumboproducts.com
Subject: RE: Mike - I need your help

Sure thing boss! How can I help?

Mike

To: mike@jumboproducts.com
From: John-jumbo@gmail.com
Subject: RE: Mike - I need your help

Here is what I want you to do for me because I'm
a little busy right now. I have been working on
incentives and I want to surprise our diligent
staff with gift cards this week. This should be
confidential until they all have the gift cards. It
is a surprise, and you will keep one for yourself
too. Can you get this done? How soon?

John

To: John-jumbo@gmail.com
From: mike@jumboproducts.com
Subject: RE: Mike - I need your help

Definitely! How many and for how much?

Mike

To: mike@jumboproducts.com
From: John-jumbo@gmail.com
Subject: RE: Mike - I need your help

I need 6 $100 eBay gift cards. You can get them at Target, CVS, 7-Eleven or any local store around or online. After you get them, scratch the back and take a clear picture of each card and send them to me on here. Please keep the physical cards and receipt for reference purposes. I will reimburse you $700.

John

Next thing you know, Mike is asking John for his $700 reimbursement, and the two eventually figure out what happened. Mike is out $600 because the cybercriminal claimed all the gift cards already and John has an employee who he's not sure he can trust anymore. The school district that lost $2.3 million made headlines, and only the town where Jumbo Products is located even know they exist. The amount of effort required to scam someone through a highly targeted social engineering attack is minimal. It does not require a large investment on the bad actors' side or the coordination of many moving pieces. The bad actors can turn your internal resources into pawns who can wreak havoc on your organization.

On other occasions, internal threats are caused by the malicious intent of an insider. These individuals are referred to as turncloaks. They abuse their power and access for a malicious purpose. Sometimes this is done for personal gain, while other times the turncloaks are coerced into it by another bad actor. An example of this would be an employee who has fallen on hard times financially and receives an offer from a bad actor to compensate them for providing data.

While not as common as pawns in phishing scams, these problems do occur and need to be on the organization's radar. One of the biggest problems with breaches caused by turncloaks is that they are hard to detect, since the employee uses access to data and systems that they have been granted permission to. While the underlying intention remains unknown, in 2018, Tesla, the US-based electric car company, experienced a data breach caused by an insider. The employee used his access to steal a large amount of sensitive information and send it to unknown third parties. There has been speculation that he did this for revenge because he did not receive a promotion; another rumor is that he did this because he was bribed by an outsider. The perpetrator later claimed to be a whistleblower. Regardless of the intent or cause, Tesla experienced a data breach that can be experienced by any organization; the transmission of data to unauthorized third parties for the gain of an individual.

External Threats

External threats and internal threats have become interwoven by using pawns and the actions of turncloaks. However, true external threats are still a major concern for organizations of any size. When I talk about external threats, I am referring to the malicious activity of an outside individual or group of individuals taking advantage of an organization's security vulnerabilities for their own benefit. Sometimes these are carried out for financial gain, and others, in the words of Bruce Wayne's butler Alfred Pennyworth, because "some men just want to watch the world burn."

Most external threats are technical in nature, and this is not the time nor place to dive into those details. For this book, I want to look at two different types of external threats: targeted and automated. While it does occur, most small businesses are far more likely to be on the receiving end of an automated attack than a targeted attack. I will use the SolarWinds hack that I referenced previously as an example of a targeted attack. The malicious actors, in this case reported to be Russian hackers, knew their targets, and worked to identify and later manipulate a security vulnerability that would allow them access to the specific groups they were targeting. You might not be on Russia's radar, but that does not mean these attacks do not happen to smaller organizations. In fact, an entire marketplace exists that allows individuals with little technical ability to cause a large impact on the target of their choice for only a small fee. We will look at West Ada School District in Idaho as an example. In 2015, a 17-year-old high school student was blamed for an attack that caused lost data during state testing, resources for online classes to be unavailable, and a general inability for computer systems to operate for nearly a week. Officials claimed the student paid a third party to perform the attack.

While targeted attacks are always a possibility, automated attacks are more likely to pose a threat to your organization. In these attacks malicious actors use automation to scour the internet for potentially vulnerable systems. Once a system is found, the system automatically starts attacking it, using known security vulnerabilities to attempt to gain access. Once the bad actor has access to the system, they have several different avenues in which they can use these computers for their own benefit. Some examples of these are **botnets, cryptojacking** and **ransomware**.

A **botnet** is a group of computers that are under the control of a bad actor. The bad actor can use the computers for several different purposes, such as sending spam emails or performing what is called a Distributed Denial-of-Service attack (DDoS). I won't go into spam emails; we are all too familiar with these. A DDoS on the other hand is an interesting attack that I think is worth having a basic understanding of.

When a DDoS attack is launched, all the computers that are part of the botnet (the bots) start sending some sort of data to a specific target. This overloads the target so that it is unable to perform its basic duties. While you may not be the target of the DDoS, your hacked computer may be participating in an attack. This is the type of attack used by the 17-year-old in Idaho to stop the school district's computers from working properly for a week. It is common for cybercriminals to build an army of bots, a botnet, then sell the ability to have their botnet perform an action, like a DDoS towards the customer's target.

Cryptojacking became a popular use of hacked systems in 2017 as the prices of cryptocurrencies, like the popular Bitcoin, soared. There are two ways you can obtain cryptocurrency: buy it from someone or do what is called mining. Mining for cryptocurrency is the process of solving complex math problems. These math problems cannot be solved by hand and require the resources of a computer to spend time solving them. Once the problem is solved, the user is rewarded with a 'coin'. As more 'coins' are mined, the math problems get harder and harder. What used to only take a relatively small amount of computational power now requires a lot of computer power.

Over time, the cost of electricity to run computers for this purpose started to add up and become expensive. Enter cryptojacking. Rather than buy computers and pay for the electric bill to mine for cryptocurrency, hackers started using the computers they had gained access to, to do this for them. They did not have to pay for the hardware or the electricity, yet they would obtain these valuable digital coins by using the hacked computers to mine for them.

When cryptojacking became popular, it was a bit of cynical relief. While no one wanted to have their computers hacked, the hackers were not wreaking havoc on the organizations they had gained access to - they were simply stealing computational power and electricity. Don't get me wrong, it was still awful, but we saw a reduction in one of the most terrifying and crippling attacks to ever happen: **ransomware**.

Before we dive into ransomware, I want to provide some background on data encryption, as it is one of the greatest things to happen in modern technology. Through the process of encrypting computer data, we can make it so someone can obtain the data as it is stored on a computer but have no ability to do anything useful with it. For example, if my banking information is all in a document that is encrypted and I send it to you, you have no way to get my actual banking information without the encryption key that only I have. The use of encryption has created a whole new level of security protection. Unfortunately, this incredibly valuable technology is now being used against us, in the form of ransomware.

In a ransomware attack, a bad actor gains access to a computer, uses a program to encrypt all the data on that computer, and then informs the user their data has been encrypted. Only the bad actor has the key to unencrypt the data, and they hold the key for ransom until they are paid. In 2015 the cybersecurity world cringed when, according to Sophos[5], a British security software and hardware company, Joseph Bonavolonta, Assistant Special Agent in charge of the Cyber and Counterintelligence Program in the FBI's Boston office, said, "The ransomware is that good... To be honest, we often advise people to just pay the ransom." Since then, the FBI has taken a clear stance, and their website now reads,[6] "The FBI does not support paying a ransom in response to a ransomware attack. Paying a ransom does not guarantee you or your organization will get any data back. It also encourages perpetrators to target more victims and offers an incentive for others to get involved in this type of illegal activity." In July 2020 it was reported that Garmin paid a $10 million ransom after their services were taken down by the WastedLocker ransomware attack. While this report has been disputed, Lawrence Abrams of BleepingComputer, a highly regarded website covering technology and cybersecurity news, noted,[7] "To obtain a working decryption key, Garmin must have paid the ransom to the attackers. It is not known how much was paid, but as previously stated, an employee had told BleepingComputer that the original ransom demand was for $10 million."

With the barrier to entry for someone to become a cybercriminal being so low, the size of a target no longer needs to be massive for them to receive a payout that is worth their investment. With this, small organizations are no longer safe to fly under the radar.

Ransomware payments and threats have increased exponentially during the Covid-19 pandemic, through increased security vulnerability from employees working remotely. In Chapter 10 we provide detailed solutions to the security risks of remote working.

SYSTEM FAILURE

The third and final risk category I want to cover is hardware and system failure. While security threats and attacks dominate the headlines, system failures continue to cause major problems for organizations of all sizes. With all our critical data being stored digitally, we run the risk of losing it all because of something as miniscule as a bad hard drive or computer part. This can happen to a single laptop with an employee's files on it, or an entire network worth of data. It might not even mean losing data but losing time. On October 1, 2020, disaster struck for Koichiro Miyahara[8], the head of the Tokyo Stock Exchange (TSE). Trading halted for an entire day. The glitch was the result of a hardware problem. Even worse, there was a subsequent failure switching over to TSE's backups. While a one-day outage at your and my organization might not have a global financial impact, it is certain to have an impact on us and our employees. If the TSE is not above a hardware failure, are we?

Before you start searching Amazon for stone tablets and chisels, I want you to know there is light at the end of this tunnel. The remainder of this book outlines how you, as a non-technical individual, can oversee and ensure your organization's IT is being managed properly. You will need to have the right people doing the work, but you will know what needs to be done. You will have the knowledge to ensure it is being done right. Best of all, you will be able to sleep better at night, because you know your organization will be there when you walk in the door the next morning.

CHAPTER SUMMARY

» Technology provides us the ability to function at great capacities and capabilities, but it presents a risk itself. The risks are associated with employee mistakes, cybersecurity threats and failure of hardware and software systems.

» User error and poor cybersecurity practices account for most mistakes that cause lost data and productivity. Regardless of how well-designed systems are, people make mistakes, and they can result in catastrophic problems.

» Security threats come both externally and internally. While we typically think of hackers as hoodie-wearing bad guys, hiding in a dark room, guiding their computer like a fighter pilot guides a jet, most attacks are automated and are not targeted at a specific organization.

» External threats may cause most of the security related problems, but internal threats like disgruntled employees or ones who have been jeopardized by an outsider are more common than we want to believe.

» If mistakes or malicious actions are not the cause of a problem, it could be as simple as a hardware failure. No matter how good our technology has gotten, hardware and software failures continue to be a large cause of downtime and data loss.

» Between user errors, malicious attacks and hardware failures, the technology used to improve the work we do also presents large risks to the wellbeing of our organizations. While these risks are real, there are great ways to mitigate the risks to protect your organization.

Chapter 2:
THE CIO

I am guessing you do not have a large C-Suite in your organization. Heck, you might not have anyone in your organization whose title starts with a C. We do not at Chartered Technology. However, I am pretty sure you have someone in charge of your organization - a CEO, whether you call them that or not. I would also venture to say that you have someone responsible for overseeing your finances - a Chief Financial Officer or CFO. You probably even have someone who oversees operations who could arguably be named the Chief Operating Officer or COO.

Regardless of title, these roles are served within your organization one way or another. It may be that one individual wears many of these hats, or that you have outsourced a role such as the CFO to a company that specializes in managing finances. Not having these responsibilities taken care of would be unthinkable and obviously irresponsible. So, who is your Chief Information Officer? Who is responsible for wearing that hat?

If you are like most organizations, you are not only without an individual in the CIO role; there is not anyone on your team who is truly playing the part either. We know someone needs to be in charge. We know someone needs to make sure our organizations can financially function, and we know someone must oversee the operations. Yet many organizations take their information, data, and technical systems for granted, and expect them to serve the organization without any leadership. I assure you this is as equally irresponsible as leaving your finances to "work themselves out" or assigning the role of financial management to an employee who "knows a lot about finance", because they have their own credit card and know how to write a check.

A significant amount of your ability to function relies on technology and the ability to use your digitally stored information. Yet, many organizations let "Joe who works in finance" oversee their technology because he is "good at computers". Joe may be awesome at computers, but just like personal finance management does not directly translate to proper payroll tax management, his personal computer knowledge does not translate to business information management. Whether the role of CIO is handled internally or outsourced, someone within your management team needs to know what the CIO's role is. Someone needs to know how to manage or oversee the person or company in the CIO role, and how to measure their success. Playing the waiting game to find out if your technology systems are being managed correctly is not an option. By the time you find out this is deficient, it may be too late.

The CIO's job is to ensure that technology and computer systems are in place to support the organization in achieving its goals. Well-run organizations view their IT this way. I can spot a well-run organization by looking at how their IT is managed. Unfortunately, a lot of organizations view IT as a utility, like water or electric service. They pay their bill and expect the water to come out of the faucet when they turn it on, and they file a service request when it does not: "It doesn't matter how the water gets to that faucet, just make it happen, and make it happen now!" While Alaska Senator Ted Stevens incorrectly referred to the internet as a "series of tubes", your IT systems are a lot more complex than that. To ensure productivity and minimize risks, these complex systems require a methodical approach to make sure they function properly and can continue to function properly for the long run.

What follows is the essential information you need to know to ensure your organization is managing technology properly. It is non-technical but will give you the knowledge to manage your IT employees or your IT vendor. It will allow you to ensure your IT is being managed properly. Make no mistake, there is a lot more to being the CIO of a Fortune 500 company than what I am providing here. But that is not what you are after, or what your organization needs. This is.

THE RESPONSIBILITIES OF A CIO

The CIO is responsible for overseeing IT expenses and budgeting, managing third-party vendors, and managing the IT team and their projects. Here is a brief overview of each of these responsibilities. The following chapters will provide a deeper dive into how each of these is managed properly.

Expenses & Budgeting

Far too many organizations are reactionary when it comes to spending money on technology. Reactionary spending in IT is a symptom of a larger problem. It means a plan is not in place. It means the organization is managing its IT with hopes and wishes. I assure you that such methods will fail you in terms of actual IT success, but they will also break the bank. Unexpected IT expenses are not only costly in terms of cash out the door, but they signify something is broken, which is likely causing productivity loss and stress among your team. IT expenses must be planned for systematically and budgeted for.

Vendor Management

If you were to print a list of vendors, it would probably be pretty long. Most small- to medium-sized organizations rely on a large number of external vendors. These vendors provide things like the materials needed to make a product, the software used to manage your daily operations, and the telephone service needed to communicate internally and with clients. They are frequently tied into your IT systems, or even are part of your IT systems. Vendors all need their systems to work, but rarely have concern for how it may impact other vendors or other systems you use. Someone needs to be managing your vendors to ensure they provide your organization what you need, and to ensure one of them does not cause problems for another vendor or system you rely on.

IT Management

To manage an IT team or vendor, it is critical you have a basic understanding of what an IT team should be working on. Management frequently views IT as the ones who fix problems. While technical support is a component to professionally managed IT, there are many areas of IT that must be in place and must be managed properly. These are:

- » Monitoring & Maintenance
- » System & Software Patching
- » Network & Endpoint Security
- » Policies & Training
- » Data Backup & Business Continuity and Disaster Recovery (BCDR)
- » Cloud Services
- » Remote Workforce
- » Technical Support

Monitoring & Maintenance

Proper IT management means proper maintenance of software, hardware and data, as well as proper monitoring of these systems to ensure they are functioning properly. Think about your car. You know to do things like change the oil and replace your tires. Like cars, tech systems need to be properly maintained to keep them operational and the overall cost of ownership down. Have you ever had your check-engine light come on? While it might not be the most helpful light, it does let you know that something is not right, and that you need to take the car to someone who can figure out what is wrong. Just like your car reports a problem or something that may become a large problem, computers frequently 'know' something is wrong before the person using them does. By monitoring computers, technicians are notified of the issue, much like your car notifies you with the check-engine light. Just like knowing there is a problem with your oil pressure before your engine blows up, you can often identify and resolve computer problems before your computer, well, blows up.

System & Software Patching

Patching is a fancy word for updating. There are two types of updates worth noting: security updates and feature updates. Both are incredibly important to manage. Ensuring security problems are fixed by security updates is an essential part of securing your IT. Thoroughly testing and vetting feature updates is critical. When they work correctly, they provide wonderful new features and capabilities that can be incredibly helpful to your users. Unfortunately, they do not always work the way they should. Far too frequently they have the opposite effect and break things that are working just fine. We will leave the technical side of this to the technical individuals, but I will provide you the information so you can understand the methodology behind when, why, and how to ensure patching is being done properly.

Network & Endpoint Security

Ensuring that both your computer network and your endpoints, a fancy word for things like computers and other network-connected devices like printers, are secure, is critical to keeping your organization operational. Just like patching, I'll spare you the technical details, but will help you understand, from a managerial perspective, what should be in place and what to look for to ensure it is being done correctly.

Policies & Training

In 2013, I watched my two-year-old zip through an iPad to get to a game like she had done it a thousand times before. Sure, she had used it a time or two, but the iPad was still pretty new to her. Apple had nailed the user interface. They had made it so intuitive that a young child could pick it up and do what they wanted to do - without being taught. While many of the programs we use today could learn a lesson or two on design from Apple, they are generally pretty easy to use. We spend a little time training our new employees on what to do, then it is off to the races. We assume that if they know technically how to use the software, then they know how we expect them to use it. For example: of course, our employees know not to use their own personal Dropbox for business. Why wouldn't they? They must know that using their personal computer to edit that new client contract is not okay - right? You know your employees can spot a phishing email, and would never actually click a link to reset their password without a deep dive into the header of the email... or would they?

The reality is that people are hard-wired to take the path of least resistance and will not even think about the potential impact their actions may have on the organization. Oftentimes that will jeopardize the security and integrity of your organization. This can be remediated through a designed program to inform employees of policies, have them sign off on those policies, and ensure they are adequately trained in how they can help prevent a cyber incident.

Data Backup & Disaster Recovery

If you understand paying for auto insurance, then you understand paying for data backup and disaster recovery systems. Sometimes problems are flat out bigger than we can handle, and the ability to go back in time can give us a second chance. I'll dig into methods to ensure you have what you need when an employee makes a simple mistake, or a true disaster strikes.

Remote Workforce

In January of 2020, some organizations had remote employees or even ran entirely virtual offices, but many still relied heavily on their physical office space. Having a remote workforce was intriguing, but many organizations held the belief that they were unique and could not operate this way. A short two months later, the world changed. Employers were forced to set employees up to work remotely. As I watched this transition, both with our clients and with businesses across the globe, I saw 'the light' finally come on. They began to see that they could operate efficiently with remote employees. The fears that productivity would nosedive were not playing out. Organizations were still functioning, and not only were many of them doing just fine, but they were also thriving. It was fun to watch this transition, but I also knew there were new problems being created. As IT departments and vendors scrambled to set employees up to work remotely, they created massive security holes in their networks and systems. They "didn't have time" to set their networks up right, so they opened their networks for remote employees to connect in, leaving massive holes in their cyber security defense.

A remote workforce can be a powerful force, but it must be managed properly. Someone within your organization needs to have a good understanding of how your employees access your data and systems to work remotely, to oversee the transition and keep a watchful eye on it moving forward.

Technical Support

Until AI takes over and we are all out of a job, people will continue to be the ones telling computers what to do. And as long as that is the case, we are going to break stuff, or at very least mess it up a little. Technical support is our saving grace. When the computer will not do what we want it to do, we know who to call. Whether they are internal or external, someone within your organization needs to manage this team. The problem is, without a technical background, it can be hard to know if they are doing the right thing. If the technical team is an outsourced vendor, it can be hard to know if you are being taken advantage of or not when it comes to billing. As we dive into the different areas you will oversee for your organization, I will show you what to be looking for to make sure your team is getting what they need, and that the IT people are doing what they are supposed to.

The idea that so many organizations leave this all to fate is terrifying. Sure, one person needs to understand what is needed for proper IT management, but that person does not have to be a technical whiz. That person just needs to care about their organization's longevity and know what to look for. Assuming you care about the longevity of your organization, the following chapters will take care of the rest for you.

CHAPTER SUMMARY

» A Chief Information Officer or CIO is responsible for ensuring that technology and computer systems are in place to support the organization in achieving its goals. Most small- to medium-sized organizations do not have anyone in this position. Leaving this role empty could be as detrimental as not having someone in charge of finances or operations.

» To fill this role, it is common to outsource it to an external IT vendor. Whether this position is housed internally or externally, someone within your organization needs to ensure this work is being done and keep tabs on it.

» The tasks involved range from expense management and budgeting to ensuring proper technology monitoring and maintenance functions are in place.

» The person you have overseeing your IT does not need to be involved in day-to-day technical operations or even have the ability to perform these tasks. They need to understand your organization's goals, what the technology-based risks are and have a general understanding of the solutions that should be in place to mitigate them.

Speaking Their Language | Rob Protzman

Chapter 3:

EXPENSE MANAGEMENT

Ask just about any department head and they will tell you that their budget is too small to accomplish the tasks they have been assigned. Ask an IT department head what they are planning on having for lunch, and they'll still spend time telling you that their budget is too small to accomplish the tasks they have been assigned. The truth is that they are probably right. IT budgeting and spending is often handled very poorly even by well-run organizations.

I rarely meet a prospective client who has a great handle on their IT spending and budgeting. They spend money on IT every year, yet they frequently lack a plan, and the money they do spend on IT often comes as a surprise. The only explanation I have come up with so far is that the lack of understanding of their IT leads to a lack of proper financial planning for it. I want you to have a firm grasp of projected costs for your IT. To understand how to properly budget for it, we will look at the following three things:

1. Business IT spending trends in the US.
2. The areas to budget for.
3. Tools you can use to help project expenses for years to come.

IT SPENDING TRENDS

I have seen several ways to come up with IT budgets, but the most accurate method I have come across is based on percentages of revenue. As businesses grow and revenues increase, so do their IT expenses, and the correlation is pretty spot on. Obviously, there are some unique industries that fall outside of these general rules, but they prove to be useful for the majority. As identified by Boardish, the developers of a risk quantification tool designed to improve the IT and cyber budgeting and sales process, the percentage of revenue is dependent on business size. Small and medium businesses, those with fewer than 100 employees, spend 6.9% of revenue on IT. Midsize businesses, those with between 100-999 employees, spend 4.1%, and large businesses, ones who have more than 1,000 employees, spend 3.2%.

As businesses grow substantially, their overall revenue percentage that is spent on IT decreases due to economies of scale. For small businesses, almost 7% of their revenue is budgeted for IT. With so many things we rely on going digital, it is important to identify what areas of expenditure should in fact be ascribed to IT. Just because it plugs in, does not necessarily mean it needs to be taken out of the IT budget. *I am looking at you Mr. Business Manager who just categorized the space heater as an IT expense...* (and yes, I've really seen that done!).

According to *The 2021 State of IT* report released by Spiceworks, a professional network for those in the information technology industry, there have been some subtle but important shifts to IT budgeting over the last few years. They have broken IT budgets into 4 categories, ranked in order of largest expense:

1. Hardware
2. Software
3. Hosted/Cloud Services
4. Managed Services

Hardware remains the largest area of IT expense, but as it pertains to the percentage of IT budgets, the expenses required for hardware are definitely shrinking, as we see the solutions we rely on move off-site to cloud-hosted systems and Software as a Service (SaaS). We see these shifts when we compare 2019 to 2021 budgets:

	2019	2021
Hardware	35%	31%
Software	26%	29%
Hosted/Cloud Services	21%	24%
Managed Services	14%	16%
Other	4%	0%

While spending on hardware is decreasing, costs are shifting into software, hosted/cloud services, and the managed services needed to properly secure and maintain these solutions. Let's take a look at how these break down for a business. In this example, we will take another look at Jumbo Products.

Jumbo Products generates $3M in gross revenue. They have 30 employees, fit into the category of a small/medium business, and have budgeted 6.9% of their revenue, or $207K for IT expenses. Their 2021 IT budget looks like this:

» Hardware: $64,170
» Software: $60,030
» Hosted/Cloud Services: $49,680
» Managed Services: $33,120

While the Software and Hosted/Cloud Services are going to look different across industries due to different back-end needs, we will look in more detail at Hardware and Managed Services, which are largely consistent across industries.

Hardware

Hardware continues to rank as the largest percentage of IT budgets; yet so many businesses are caught off guard when these expenses come up. Fortunately, predicting hardware expenses is one of the easiest things to do and to budget for. Before we get into the budgeting process, let's take a look at hardware lifecycles. By this I mean, specifically, the life expectancy of computers.

Predicting the lifespan of a computer is easy. By looking at hardware failure rates in comparison to the age of a computer, we can decide how long we should anticipate keeping that computer. In general, computers have roughly a 4.5% failure rate after the first year. When we get into years four through five, that rate jumps up to almost 25%. While it may seem obvious, as computers age, they fail more frequently. With failures come not only the cost of replacement, but many additional costs as well.

Before Jumbo Products had a good hardware budget and computer replacement plan, one of their product designers, Susan, was using a five-year-old computer. Jumbo Products probably should have replaced the computer after it was four years old and the hard drive had failed; but after the failure, Jumbo was able to replace the hard drive for $275, including parts and labor. Susan kept on using the computer.

Leading up to that hard drive failure, Susan was struggling for about 6 weeks to get her job done. Her computer kept crashing or just plain running slow. On average, Susan lost about an hour each day while she was watching a spinning wheel as her programs loaded and rebooted multiple times. Not only did Susan lose time, but the slow computer made her agitated; her overall performance went down. Susan missed a few deadlines, leading to one of Jumbo's new products being delayed by two weeks. While we do not know how much that delay cost Jumbo Products, we can easily add up the costs of repair and the amount Susan, who makes $25 an hour, was paid while she was unable to work. Susan's five-year-old computer cost the company at least $1,025 - and after spending that money, Susan *still* had an old computer.

It is pretty tempting to delay large capital expenditures like computer replacements, but the numbers do not lie. It simply costs more money to keep old computers around than it does to replace them. While somewhat difficult to quantify, it is undeniable that employees lose productivity not only because of poor computer performance, but also due to frustration with their old computers. Businesses need to get in the habit of replacing computers before they fail. Over time, a computer replacement plan saves money and may even keep that great employee from walking out the door. Based on hardware failure rates, I recommend planning replacements based on the following lifespans:

» Laptops: 3 years
» Desktops: 4 years
» Servers: 5 years

Let's take a look at Jumbo Products' computer replacement plan. They have a total of 36 computers. For the sake of simplicity, let's say they are all laptops and get replaced after being used for three years. Jumbo has dedicated 40% of their hardware budget for annual computer replacements; the rest is reserved for things like servers, network equipment, printers, office phones and cell phones. Computers for their designers cost about $5K each, while the rest of their laptops cost about $2K each. All in all, Jumbo has about $110K worth of laptops, with each computer averaging a $2,100 replacement cost. Based on their replacement cycle, Jumbo needs to replace 12 laptops each year. They spend $25,200 to do this, which keeps them within their budget of $26,668.

Developing a computer replacement plan is easy. I have developed a Computer Replacement Schedule & Budget Calculator that I will gladly give you for free. You can get it by visiting `www.speakingtheirlanguage.com/calculator`.

Managed Services

Looking at the IT budget areas listed above, you will notice that there is not a line item for an IT department. Most small- to medium-sized businesses have made the decision to outsource their IT management rather than keep it in house; this shows up in the budget under 'managed services.' When you look at the percentage for 2021, you will see that managed services are only 16% of the budget. For our friends at Jumbo Products, that means they have about $33K budgeted.

As an employer, you know that you cannot hire an IT person for $33K, let alone a department. By outsourcing IT to a Managed Service Provider (MSP), you can keep a big chunk of your IT budget for things like hardware, software and hosted/cloud services. It really does not make sense to eat up half or more of your IT budget on internal staffing.

Most Managed Service Providers will charge for their services by billing per user or per computer. For Jumbo Products, their MSP bills per user. Jumbo can comfortably budget $92 per user, per month, for their managed IT. If you already have a MSP, you know that budget is pretty low; but keep in mind that the amount you pay your MSP per user also includes the costs for some of your hosted and cloud services such as email and file storage. That is the case for Jumbo Products. They pay their MSP $175 per user per month which includes quite a few items that would normally fall into their hosted and cloud services budget. This leaves Jumbo with around $19K remaining in the hosted/cloud services budget to pay for services like their Manufacturer Resource Planning product that is specific to their industry.

One of the keys to IT success is proactive budgeting and planning. It is easy to see IT only as a cost; but the reality is that IT plays a large role in generating revenue and must be treated as such. Letting employees use computers until those computers die not only kills morale, but it can also break the bank. Your IT expenses are real, so your budgeting and planning for them should be too.

CHAPTER SUMMARY

» Every year money is spent to acquire, repair, and maintain technology, yet these expenses are often poorly managed and come as a surprise.

» With the right tools, your organization can get a handle on these expenses, so they are well thought out and your money goes further.

» Using the provided data for similar sized organizations will give you an idea of how much should be spent on technology and in what areas.

» Hardware continues to be the largest expense for most organizations followed by software, hosted/cloud services, and managed services. Use the free computer replacement schedule and budget calculator I have provided to forecast your hardware purchasing.

» Having a well-developed plan for these expenses is not difficult. It will result in a long-term cost savings and provide for more reliable and sustainable technology.

Chapter 4:

VENDOR MANAGEMENT

Take a few minutes to jot down the names of the vendors who provide you with software and the equipment that connects to your computer network. If you are like most businesses, you will have a pretty long list. These vendors include companies who provide you services like Voice over IP (VoIP) phone services, printers and copiers, inventory control software, customer relationship management software and accounting software. If you keep thinking about your list, you will find that you also have an internet service provider, an alarm system you can control from your smartphone, a video surveillance system, and maybe even a solution for digital display boards.

Every one of these solutions has found its way into your world and onto your network for one reason or another. Checking in on your building when you are not there through the video surveillance system affords you peace of mind. When you are not in the office but need to make a work call, you can make it look like the call is coming from your work phone. No matter how much we try to go digital, we still all need to print things from time to time. The tech-enabled tools available to us now are incredibly useful. Outsourcing the management and maintenance of these systems allows you to take advantage of the technology while keeping them affordable.

All these vendors want their specific products to work great for you; however, they rarely have concerns about how well other vendors' solutions work in relation to theirs. Vendors operate in silos, without regard for the impact their solution may have on another vendor's product, or even your underlying network.

At the point of installation, you want them to get their job done and be on their way. When the copier company comes to install that fancy new multifunction printer/scanner/copier/cappuccino machine and they tell you they need to install some software on your server, you get them logged in and let them loose. An hour or so after these printer people leave, you get a call from the production department saying that their label printer will not work anymore.

After you bang your head against the wall a few times, you realize the only thing that has changed is the new copier in the sales office. It could not be that though - they did not do anything to the production label printers. Right? The new copier is working great for your sales team, and the copier guy is long gone. The printer for your production team is not even managed by the copier guys. That printer comes from the vendor who provides your inventory management software. Who do you call? Whose problem is it?

Well, it is your problem. The copier guy did his job, and when you call him, he reminds you that they do not manage the label printer. The inventory management vendor did not change anything. How long are you going to have to wait on hold to find the support engineer who can find and fix the problem with your label printer?

Have you ever made the decision to keep something around - like an old copier or phone system - that does not work well and needs to be poked in the right place every now and then just to keep it running? This situation is not great; but the last time you made a big change like that, so many things broke that you figure it is just not worth replacing the malfunctioning piece again. Then you feel stressed, out of control, and stuck with a faulty system.

Allowing outsiders to make decisions or changes that serve only their solution and end up causing problems for other parts of your organization should not be the norm. The vendor responsible for making sure the new phone system gets set up correctly is not responsible for making sure all your technology works together; nor should they bear the burden of a problem the phone system causes to a whole other system on your network.

All these technical problems, frustrations and concerns are a result of poor vendor management. When we have different individuals exclusively responsible for different parts of our systems, we experience these types of problems. Implementing a vendor management program will allow your organization to make the additions and changes you need without having to worry if they will break more things than they will fix.

A proper vendor management program has 3 components:
1. A central point of contact for all external vendors
2. A change management process
3. A system for documentation

Centralized Point of Contact
The centralized point of contact is not responsible for knowing every system in detail. Having a single point of contact does not mean shifting the management of all systems to one person. Instead, this point of contact is the gatekeeper. They are the ones who develop relationships with all your vendors. When the sales team wants to start using some new software, they bring the centralized point of contact into the conversation early, before any changes or decisions are made. The point of contact does not need

to be the one negotiating the deal with the vendor or determining how effective the solution is, but they need to be in the know. When it comes time for implementation, the point of contact will ensure that there has been coordination between the new vendor, internal departments and other vendors that may be impacted.

Change Management

A change management process allows for changes to be reviewed before they are made. It sounds simple, and it really is. However, you will find that most vendors do not normally go through this process. They know their plan, but it typically is along the lines of: "We install these things all the time, it will be fine." (You will notice there is no plan because many vendors do not believe they need one for standard operation.) On top of all the benefits having a vendor management plan provides to your organization in the long run, it also frequently makes for a significantly better implementation. By going through the change management plan, vendors and decision makers are forced to review what they are doing. Often, they come up with a better way to do things than they have in the past. A good change management plan has six components:

1. Plan for change
2. Reason for change
3. Completed testing
4. Potential impacts
5. Rollback strategy
6. Approval process

The **plan for change** is simply a documented explanation of what changes are going to be made. This should include a detailed explanation of what changes are going to be made, the *order* in which they are going to be made, and the *timeline* for when they are going to be made. By developing a detailed explanation for changes, not only will the process be decided and easy to follow when it comes time to make the change; the individuals who are responsible for the change management plan often find problems that may have occurred and are able to account for them ahead of time.

While it may seem elementary to require someone looking to make a change to provide these details, this process provides an opportunity for the person writing it to review logically if the change is even necessary, and then document a clear **reason for change**. Between great marketing campaigns and manufacturer reps who like to take your team out for beers and a round of *Top Golf*, there are many, many changes that get proposed for the wrong reasons. Having a team member write out the reason for change in detail allows them to review how much the change is needed and provide sound, detailed reasoning for it.

The third step in the change management plan is **testing**. By performing testing ahead of time, many problems can be avoided. The testing process allows for changes to be made in the implementation plan that will identify and help avoid potential hiccups and make for a better result in the end. Depending on the magnitude of the change, an entire testing environment or sandbox may be worth developing to help finalize the plan for change.

A simpler test could look like this: test the change on one user on whom it will have minimal impact if it does not work correctly. If this goes well, roll out the change to the whole office. When a detailed list of testing procedures is provided in the change management plan, the organization can be relatively confident that the solution will work when the time comes to go live.

Just like a new copier in the sales office can impact the functioning of a label printer, it is important to identify and document which systems may be impacted by the proposed change. At this point, assume that nothing will go right and potentially *anything* could go wrong. Think laterally and in unexpected places! Whilst the department head and vendor may just be looking to add a new digital display board in the entryway, that display board could impact how the security system and network run. By identifying these potential snags ahead of time, the problems can be avoided when it comes time to make the change.

Ensure there is a **rollback strategy** in place, to allow for a quick and easy return to normal operations if things do not go well during a change. An example of this is having a plan in place to return a server back to the way it was operating before a major software upgrade is done. While the software upgrade should go smoothly, there is always a chance that things can go wrong. What may have been a planned server outage for 30 minutes could end up being an outage for hours or even days while you try to undo the work that caused the problem. With a well-developed rollback strategy, a plan is already in place to get things operational if the upgrade causes problems. When these problems occur, tensions can run high, and people often start acting without a clear head. A well-developed rollback strategy will give you something to fall back on to put things back the way they were before the problem occurred. Having this planned out ahead of time will allow it to be done quickly, without having to come up with a fix on the spot. Believe me, this can save some sweaty palms, when all eyes are on you as the minutes tick by with the whole business at a standstill. Even if you are the one making the change, it can be highly beneficial to have a plan for you to refer to, put in place when all eyes were *not* on you, and you had the time to think through the best way to get things back to the way they were.

Simply going through the exercise of developing a change management plan will often resolve problems before they occur. Along with having a process to follow for developing this plan, it is important to define what the **approval process** is for each change management plan. This allows for key stakeholders to be on the same page and understand five things:

1. what will be happening
2. Why it will be happening
3. What has been done to ensure it will go well
4. Who needs to be involved in the discussion
5. What the plan is if things do not go as planned

I have made our Change Management Plan template available for free at www.speakingtheirlanguage.com/ changemanagement. Download it now so you can start using it right away.

Documentation

Documentation is key. You have heard it before, and you will hear it again. A good vendor management program involves a well-designed documentation system. Maintaining good documentation for vendor management allows the point of contact to access information easily. This can save the whole organization time and ensure you have what you need when you need it.

While each vendor will be somewhat unique, the basic things that should be documented for all vendors include this reasonably detailed and comprehensive list:

» the vendor's name
» account number
» sales contact information
» billing contact information
» technical contact information
» who in your organization is their main contact
» a list of systems and/or other vendors they integrate with
» agreement value
» agreement start and end dates
» an overview of their services
» details of their services
» a record of communication and work performed

Do not bother creating your own documentation template for this; go to www.speakingtheirlanguage.com/vendortemplate for a free template you can start using right away.

Managing vendors involves much more than getting their bills paid on time - but it need not be overly complex. Spending some time documenting vendors in this way will save you so much time in the future... and many potential headaches. You may or may not end up being the point of contact for your organization - but someone needs to be. Using the free tools I have provided will make it so easy to get started.

The next several chapters deal with technical areas of managing IT within your organization. Again, I assure you this is not a technical manual. You will need a team of trained IT personnel to implement and manage these items, and this will provide you a good understanding of what needs to be done and why.

CHAPTER SUMMARY

» External vendors are a key component to every organization. Having these vendors keeps costs down while allowing organizations to receive the tools and services needed to operate.

» Vendors rarely account for the impact their systems will have on others. This often causes compatibility problems.

» An established vendor management plan will help to alleviate these issues. This starts with a centralized point of contact for all vendors. This individual is not responsible for managing all vendors and all systems, but rather plays the role of gatekeeper and keeps the correct people involved.

» A change management process is critical. Going through this process prior to making a change will provide a higher likelihood of success while avoiding interruption of other systems outside of the vendor's scope of work.

» Maintaining good documentation for vendor management allows the point of contact to easily access information that can save the whole organization time and ensure you have what you need when you need it.

Speaking Their Language | Rob Protzman

Chapter 5:

MONITORING & MAINTENANCE

The healthcare industry has shifted from reactionary to proactive medical treatment, both to improve the lives of individuals, and to reduce their cost. Proactive monitoring and maintenance of your computer systems will allow your organization to do the same.

There are three common methods for keeping computers functioning. In the IT industry, we refer to the first one as **break/ fix**. As the name suggests, organizations use their computers; when they break, they call in the person to come fix it. The second maintenance method is more proactive; it is referred to as **scheduled maintenance**. With this method, the IT person or team will work on a computer on a scheduled basis - usually quarterly - to give it a checkup, clean it up a bit and send it on its way. The third method is **active monitoring and preventative maintenance**. Primarily through automation, active monitoring and preventative maintenance allow for problems to be detected early, often before the user knows there is a problem. With this approach, maintenance tasks are performed as needed rather than on a schedule.

So many things we do in our jobs rely on computers. Even those employees who do not work with computers frequently rely on them. The employee in the greenhouse who needs to start germinating seeds often relies on data provided by metrics determined by a computer program. The warehouse worker who moves pallets around relies on proper inventory management systems that are entirely computer-based. When computers have problems, the impact goes far beyond the person sitting at the computer managing a program. When production gets shut down, the company loses revenue. Employees are still paid while they are forced to cease working by such a shutdown, and unapplied labor costs start stacking up... fast.

The stress of computer malfunctions alone causes major issues in the workplace. When products and services cannot go out the door, management is not happy and will have some explaining to do. Employees who are just trying to do their jobs get stuck spending time fighting a computer rather than being productive. The stresses add up and have a negative impact on the organization's ability to function well.

As technology becomes more integrated into every facet of our operations, we can be more efficient and accomplish bigger and better things. Yet tech we put into place to help us can, when it malfunctions, also be the thing that completely halts our ability to operate. It is just plain wrong to allow these tools that promise so much to be the thing that shut us down, just because they are not properly cared for.

Many organizations still rely on a break/fix model of IT management. Management adopts this model in a belief that it will reduce costs. The reality is, break/fix ends up costing *more*, all while yielding bad results. The situation instantly becomes stressful when a system breaks down. The employee or employees who rely on it lose productivity while they wait for it to get fixed; meanwhile they are still getting paid to be at work. The organization loses revenue as productivity halts. In a rush to get back up and running, the fastest solution is put into place. This solution often does not resolve the underlying problem and the issue comes back.

This cycle continues as money is paid out hourly to the 'IT Guy' who rushes over to metaphorically put out the fire. While I disagree with the proposition offered by IT companies that offer a break/fix option, the real problem rests with the organizations who hire them. These organizations allow this type of model to be offered by expecting a fast fix and yet are not prepared to pay to get the job done right. Frequently the break/fix bills add up during the year to the point where they show a higher cost than had things been maintained proactively. When adding up these bills, lost productivity, lost revenue and the, while unquantifiable, distress caused by operating in this manner, it flat out costs significantly more and provides you way less.

Many organizations have attempted to solve their break/fix woes by implementing a scheduled maintenance method of IT management. Scheduled maintenance is better than no maintenance at all. If you chart the effectiveness though, you will see a pattern that resembles a wave. Scheduled maintenance is usually done on a quarterly basis. At the beginning of a quarter, things are running smoothly, as maintenance has just been done. This is the crest of the wave. But immediately following the scheduled maintenance, things can only head in one direction: down. As the quarter goes on, systems begin to slow down and problems start to occur. Eventually, they hit the trough of the wave pattern as they barely scape by. As another quarter begins and scheduled maintenance is performed, the cycle continues.

In addition to the cyclical nature of IT effectiveness in a scheduled maintenance system, this approach comes with other problems. When maintenance is performed this infrequently, it takes more time. While systems are being worked on, employees are not able to get their work done. The 'IT Guy' is getting paid to work on the computer while the employee is getting paid to do nothing. Additionally, early warning signs of problems are frequently not seen before a major problem occurs. Not only does general performance decrease while heading towards the trough of the wave, but things such as indications of hardware failures go unseen, leaving a high likelihood of work-stopping problems, which then turns into break/fix problems.

The best approach to take, one that overcomes all the drawbacks of break/fix or of scheduled maintenance, is active monitoring and proactive maintenance. When active monitoring and proactive maintenance is in place, computer systems can continuously function at their highest level of performance and most major problems can be avoided due to early intervention. Through modern automation, in the form of a monitor in place in the background, this can be done with little to no impact on the user's ability to get work done. I have lost count of how many hard drives we have replaced over the years, neatly fitted in while the employee is on their lunch break. Through active monitoring we have been able to identify that their drive was about to fail and resolve the issue quickly and easily before it caused major problems for their productivity.

When monitors are in place, they can identify when a computer is headed towards a problem. This monitor can be used to trigger a maintenance task to resolve the issue before it becomes a problem. Rather than performing maintenance based on a schedule, maintenance can be completed only when needed. In the event that an automated task does not resolve the problem, a technician can be notified and given the opportunity to intervene. Here are a few examples of this at work:

Log File Monitoring
As computers perform tasks, they will frequently keep a log of the work performed. These logs can be incredibly helpful and are used

by IT support and software engineers to identify the cause of a problem if one occurs. The downside to this is that oftentimes, log files can become large and end up causing problems themselves. The problems they typically cause are filling up disk space that can lead to computer crashes, or they can become too large so that the program can no longer update them, causing the program to slow down or crash. To avoid this problem, a monitor can be set up to track the size of a log file. If the log file gets to a certain size that indicates it may start causing problems, a maintenance routine to prune or clear out the log file can be performed.

Performance Monitoring

By tracking the performance history of a computer, a baseline of 'normal' can be identified. A monitor can be set to alert the IT support team when a computer begins using more of its resources than has been determined to be 'normal.' By identifying this as it begins to happen, actions can be taken before it becomes a major problem for the user.

Some of these actions may be automated, such as finding 'stuck' or 'hung' computer processes - programs that are supposed to be running but have stopped working, causing the computer to operate below par. Automation can restart those processes so they operate as they should.

Other times, as an employee begins taking on more responsibility for an organization, they may be required to run additional programs on their computer. While the computer may have been well suited for them previously, it may need to have some upgrades to get it to serve the user in their new role. One of the items that is often identified and is incredibly inexpensive to fix is increased computer memory (or RAM) usage. As computers start to use up their available RAM, they noticeably slow down – we've all been there, right? When this happens, the performance monitor can alert a technician to the issue and allow them to add more

RAM to a computer. Rather than the user struggling with a slowed down computer and losing productivity, an upgrade can be made which can cost as little as $20. The performance improvement will be huge!

Drive Health

We've all either experienced the pain of a hard drive crash or know someone who has. Having a hard drive die in a computer creates all kinds of trouble. Storage devices like hard drives are used in every computer to save information. They are constantly reading and writing information and are in use every minute the computer is running. Hard drive/storage health is essential to getting work done.

While most modern computers use Solid State Drives (SSD), which store information similarly to a flash drive, with no moving parts, all storage devices are subject to failure. Without storage, a computer becomes totally useless. While there is not a *silver bullet* that can stop computer parts from failing, we can get pretty close by monitoring the health of computer storage. According to BackBlaze, one of the largest cloud storage and data backup providers, 76.7% of the time, storage drives will indicate a problem before they fail. This information is logged by the computer, but there must be something in place to relay this message to a technician so they can intervene. By monitoring a computer for these errors, companies can replace hard drives before they fail.

Replacing drives before they fail saves a bunch of time; information from one hard drive can simply be copied to the new drive. The alternative: a technician must rebuild the computer from the ground up when a drive fails. Not only is the process of replacing a drive before it fails much faster, but it can be scheduled to be completed while the employee is on a lunch break, as mentioned above. The employee does not lose productivity and is far less stressed than when their computer has gone kaput.

So much of the time, computers know they have problems before users do. If we are set up to listen to them, we can be proactive and keep them healthy. Our healthcare system has acknowledged that people live healthier lives with preventative care, and that prevention costs less than treatment. The same goes for our computers. They are integrated into our daily lives, and we rely on them for our organization to be successful. We can no longer treat computers like a simple one-off piece of hardware that we bandage up when there is a problem. We must be proactive to keep them working properly, keeping our users happy and our organization operational.

CHAPTER SUMMARY

» You will have better results and your money will go further by managing your IT in a proactive way.

» There are wonderful tools to allow your IT team to be far more effective than simply waiting until a user reports a problem.

» By actively monitoring computer health and performance, automation can be used to resolve common issues that would normally go unnoticed until an employee starts to lose productivity. This allows computers to run better day-to-day as issues are resolved before your employees even know they exist.

» When automation does not fix the issue or there is an indication of impending hardware failure, a technician is notified and able to intervene before it becomes a major problem.

» Reactionary IT services result in higher rates of poor performance, downtime and lost revenue. Proactive monitoring and maintenance keep things running well and your employees productive.

Chapter 6:
PATCH MANAGEMENT

Patch Management is a fancy term for having control of installing updates for software and operating systems. Companies like Microsoft and Apple release regular updates, aka patches, for their operating systems and software. These updates come in two major forms: one, feature/version updates and two, security updates. Feature and version updates include enhancements to their products, such as to the Windows or OS X operating systems. These are often enhancements to the user interface and the underlying code that makes your computer run. Meanwhile, security updates fix problems in the product that have been identified and found to be able to be exploited by cyber criminals to gain unauthorized access to your computers.

Most operating systems and software have the built-in ability to automatically install these updates for you. It is in the creators of those operating systems best interest for you to keep your system updated, especially with security updates. But while well-intentioned, and ideal for home computer use, relying on automatic updates for your organization will create major problems.

One significant problem that can occur from relying on automatic updates: a feature update is installed, and rather than providing great new features, it actually causes problems for the software you rely on to operate. Major changes in operating systems frequently cause problems with software until that software has been updated to be compatible with the new operating system update. In addition to software incompatibility, we are seeing more and more problems with basic computer functions caused by updates, as Microsoft and Apple race to push out new features. Headlines like 'New macOS update is wrecking Macbooks: what to do now' from *Laptop* magazine, or 'Microsoft is still struggling with broken Windows 10 updates' from Tech Radar are all too common. But in a perverse way, if automatic updates are *not* causing problems by installing bad updates, there is a good chance that the automatic update process is broken. If this is the case, the computer is also not receiving security updates. A quick Google search for 'broken Windows automatic updates' will return about 125 million results and 'broken Mac automatic updates' over 18 million.

Between bad updates and broken auto-update configurations, trusting the automatic update process is too risky for organizations to rely on. When you do not know any better, you may assume updates are being installed as they should be. Yet the inner voice asking, "Are our computers updated and protected?" can lead to anxiety as you read headline after headline about data breaches and cybercrime.

Hope is a bad strategy for patch management. You deserve for these tools to work properly. The reality is, you simply cannot trust them. They are supposed to work properly, but too frequently they do not.

A comprehensive patch management strategy allows for security vulnerabilities to be fixed as soon as possible while not allowing feature updates to be installed until they have been tested and confirmed to work properly in your environment. There are spectacular tools that allow this to be done properly, and your internal IT team or outsourced Managed Service Provider should have them in place. When implemented properly, it is quick and easy to see the status of security patches and feature updates across all your computers.

Determining which security updates need to be applied should be done based on the level of risk the vulnerability presents to your organization. To help organizations determine their risks, the United States government's National Infrastructure Advisory Council developed the Common Vulnerability Scoring System or CVSS. CVSS works by assigning a score ranging from 0 to 10 for a known vulnerability, with 10 being the most severe. By using the CVSS system, IT teams can prioritize their workflow based on the risk of the problem.

In addition to the CVSS score, security updates are assigned a Common Vulnerabilities and Exposures, or CVE, number. Each CVE number is unique and is used to identify publicly known vulnerabilities. A well-designed patch management system will catalog the updates that are available for your environment, track them by CVE number, and allow for automatic approval for installation based on their CVSS score.

In March of 2021, CVE-2021-26855, a vulnerability in Microsoft's Exchange Server, used for organizations to send and receive email, was identified. It was given a CVSS score of 9.1. The vulnerability was accessible over a network, required low complexity to take advantage of, and required no existing computer privileges or user interaction. It was bad, and it was being exploited by cybercriminals.

The vulnerability, along with a handful of other vulnerabilities discovered at that time, allowed attackers to gain easy access to organizations' emails. A good patch management system would have identified the patch to fix this problem when it was released, automatically approved the patch for installation, and ensured it was installed on any servers running the impacted versions of Exchange. While this specific vulnerability made headlines, there are a large amount of operating system and software vulnerabilities being released all the time. When looking at historic CVSS statistics, more than 35% of vulnerabilities have received a score of 7 or higher, indicating a high or critical severity.

Making the decision to install feature and version updates comes down to compatibility and support from the vendor. It is important to go through the change management process prior to rolling them out at a large scale, and to keep track of the vendor's support for older versions.

In an ideal world, your IT team will have what is called a sandbox in which to test updates. A sandbox is a testing environment for computers that mimics your real-world computer environment. By installing feature and version updates in the sandbox first, they can be tested before being installed for your users. However, I have yet to find a small business which has invested in a true sandbox environment - so, while this may be useful in an ideal world, it is unlikely to exist in the real world.

So, if a sandbox is not available, feature updates should be initially installed only on a subset of computers within an organization, and preferably on computers for users who do not perform business-critical functions. For example, while it may be inconvenient for the marketing person at Jumbo Products to have a computer problem due to a feature update, the organization in general will still function while the marketing person's problem is resolved. Once the feature update has been tested and confirmed to not break anything - or that the enhancements outweigh the things that it does break - the feature update can be scheduled for installation on the computers in the production department and elsewhere.

Eventually, there comes a time when feature updates must be installed. This is referred to as End of Life or EOL. After a certain period of time, vendors such as Microsoft will stop releasing security updates for older versions of their products. They reasonably expect that organizations are keeping up with updates, and they no longer devote resources to fixing bugs in older versions of their products.

EOL should not come as a surprise to the people managing your IT. These dates are announced far in advance of the products' actual EOL, often when the products or new versions were initially released. Once a software or operating system version becomes EOL, security updates are no longer released for those versions, leaving them and organizations running them vulnerable to cyberattacks. On rare occasions, vendors will release what are referred to as Out-of-Band updates.

There may be no better indication of how bad a vulnerability is than when Microsoft releases one of these. These are updates to old versions of their products that are no longer supported and often have not received any updates for years. In recent history, Microsoft has released a few high profile Out-of-Band updates, including one in 2017 for Windows XP. Windows XP had gone EOL three years earlier and was now vulnerable to a highly effective and widespread ransomware attack called WannaCry which caused an estimated $4 billion in losses globally.

Additionally, in March of 2021 Microsoft released an update for versions of Exchange server dating back to 2010, which while still in use in some places, had been EOL for quite some time in regard to the vulnerabilities mentioned at the beginning of this chapter. So, while Out-of-Band updates are made available, they are rare and should never be relied upon. It really is time to update the system!

In January of 2020, the world's most popular operating system, Windows 7, went EOL and it became time to migrate to Windows 10. In an article published by *Security Week*, Mike Puglia, who is Chief Strategy Officer at an IT infrastructure management solution provider for MSPs and IT teams called Kaseya, was quoted saying: "With the average cost per breach now standing at around $3.92 million, failure to migrate could give just one breach the power to end your business - a scary thought given that two-thirds of businesses have yet to even develop a migration strategy[...]." The article went on to paint a grim picture:

"Puglia [...]has pointed out that nearly 500 vulnerabilities were found in desktop versions of Windows in 2018 alone, and roughly 170 of them were considered critical. Moreover, Puglia noted, one in three data breaches globally is the result of unpatched vulnerabilities and, as the WannaCry incident demonstrated, organizations running unsupported versions of Windows will be hit the hardest in case of a major attack."

Identifying which patches to install and when to install them is critical. Ensuring they are actually installed is just as important. Relying on automatic updates to protect your organization is simply too risky.

A patch management system has both technical and operational components. While your technical team can and should handle the installation and monitoring of patches, the individual or MSP acting as your CIO should be assisting with the decisions being made on update approvals and the timeline for rollout.

In the next chapter we will look at the additional technical safeguards that must be in place to prevent problems even if your systems are fully patched.

CHAPTER SUMMARY

» Patch Management is a fancy term for managing operating system and software updates. These patches come in two forms, feature updates and security updates.

» Feature updates bring added functionality for the product, but often cause problems for other products and services. They should be fully tested before being installed across your organization.

» Security patches fix problems that make your organization vulnerable to malicious attacks by cybercriminals. A scoring system is in place to indicate how bad a problem is that the patch fixes. The scores can be used to prioritize the installation of patches.

» Operating systems have built in functions to automatically install patches. These can cause problems by installing feature updates before they have been tested. They are also notorious for not working well which can lead to patches not being installed when they should be.

» Patch management systems allow your IT team to decide which patches should be installed and when. They also provide centralized reporting on which computers have and have not installed patches so your IT team can intervene if there is a problem.

Chapter 7:
SECURITY –
TECHNICAL
SOLUTIONS

From data breach notifications in your inbox to news of major hacks of tech giants and our own US government, it is obvious that cybercrime is not going away any time soon. Many aspects of cybersecurity are interwoven into various areas of IT management, such as patch management. However, there are dedicated systems and tools that must be in place to keep your systems and data protected against cybercrime. These can assist in blocking any malicious activity that can cause major problems for your organization. Without getting into the technical nitty gritty of these solutions, this chapter will give you a thorough understanding of what your organization must be doing to reduce the risks of cyberattacks.

There is no 'one way' that cyberattacks can get into your systems. There are many possible entry points for these attacks. They can come through an individual computer, through your network, and through productivity systems - just to name a few. Failure to properly protect these systems can and likely will lead to an event that ranges in severity from a minor inconvenience to a loss so large that your organization will no longer remain operational. As discussed in Chapter 1, attacks that formerly required highly skilled and well-funded cybercriminal organizations are now able to be carried out by criminals with just a small amount of money and minimal computing knowledge.

Many small businesses hold the belief that they are not at risk of a cyberattack due to their size. While this may have been the case in the past, it simply is not true now. According to Verizon's 2020 Data Breach Investigation Report, nearly one third of data breaches involved small businesses. This can be attributed to the lower cost of entry for cybercriminals and the reality that small businesses can now operate like large businesses due to the availability of cloud services.

One of the things I think to myself, discuss with our team, and hear from our clients is "Why don't these guys get real jobs? If they are this good at being bad, think of the good they could do if they were acting as productive members of society!" While this would be a great turn of events, no matter how much we wish cybercriminals could turn from 'bad guys' to 'good guys', they simply do not.

There are several methods to combat cyberattacks, from utilizing tech tools to employee education. We will look at the non-technical side of combating cyberattacks in the next chapter. Here we will look at the technical methods your organization needs to have in place. Not only do these methods need to be in place, but they must be actively monitored and maintained to be effective. Simply paying for a tool or service may allow you to 'check the box' of doing something, but there must be active participation from leadership and the technical team to ensure these tools fulfil their purpose.

Much like automatic updates, trusting that security tools will do their job, by setting them and forgetting them, will frequently result in major problems. When it comes to the technical side of cybersecurity, we will look at protecting your organization at the network level, the computer level, and for your cloud-based services. While any one of these tools might be good enough to prevent an attack, it is important to have multiple layers of protection in place.

A great analogy for this is bullet-proof glass. Bullet-proof glass is made by layering different materials on top of one another. While none of them are strong enough to stop a bullet on their own, when put together they create an impenetrable barrier. While a bullet may break through the first layer or even the second or third, it will eventually be stopped before getting through. This is the theory behind multi-layered security. Trusting one system to prevent an attack is risky. By combining multiple different types of security, you are far more likely to be protected and the attack prevented.

NETWORK LEVEL PROTECTION

Network level protection involves your firewall, web filtering, Intrusion Detection Systems (IDS) and Intrusion Prevention Systems (IPS). Changes to these systems need to be well thought out and actively monitored. Making use of the change management process I detailed in Chapter 4 for changes to these systems will help to ensure any changes that are made to improve security go smoothly.

I first learned about physical firewalls while in high school, trying to earn some money over the summer. I had an opportunity to help several people protect their property in the event of an actual fire. Hang with me; I assure you these two types of firewall are related.

There were several cottages by a lake, that were physically attached; they shared a common porch and more importantly they shared a common attic space. The property owners knew that if a fire were to start in one unit, it would quickly spread to the others once it reached the attic. My job was to go into these attics and build a wall between each unit. A physical firewall. The owners had determined that installing fire resistant drywall sheets between each unit would provide the protection they needed to slow a fire from spreading.

While installing the sheets of drywall in the attic, I found that there were numerous sheets that I had to cut holes in so that things like plumbing and electrical wiring could get through between the units. While it would have been more effective against a fire to have no holes at all, tearing out the plumbing and electricals to the units would have left them useless, so the holes needed to be there. There were some old cables that were no longer in use, so rather than cut a hole in the firewall for them, I removed those cables.

Our network firewalls behave very similarly to physical firewalls. They stand between our networks and the rest of the world - a world where metaphorical fires spring up at an astonishing rate. Cutting off all connection to the outside world, much like removing the electrical wiring and plumbing from those attics, would be a highly effective protection method. Blocking all network traffic from moving through a firewall would create a very secure network. Nothing could get through to cause a problem. But, and I'm sure you're ahead of me here, if nothing can get through, the network would be useless since we rely so heavily on internet-based resources.

For us to access things like web pages, we need to allow that traffic through the firewall. Much like cutting a hole in drywall to allow an electrical wire to go through, we allow network traffic through our network firewalls so we can have the things we need to function. We must accept some level of risk to maintain the benefit of using the internet. Things change over the course of time, though. While something may have been required to get through your firewall previously, this might not be necessary anymore. Much like the old cables I removed while installing the physical firewall so it didn't have excess holes, network firewalls need to be proactively managed to ensure that the 'holes' we have opened up previously still need to be there. Proactive monitoring of your firewalls is a must, too. If a change is made that could lead to a security problem, IT personnel should be notified so it can be reviewed or disabled in a timely manner.

Websites remain one of the major entry points for malicious software. While a website may be owned by a reputable company that you conduct regular business with, it is possible for that website to be hacked and then serve up malicious content to visitors. Having a system in place to monitor website traffic in real time can prevent this malicious content from attacking your computers.

By having a solution like this in place for our clients, on numerous occasions we have been the first to inform companies that we had no previous relationship with, that their websites have been hacked. One time in particular, a client of ours, a brewery, informed us that they were being blocked from accessing their distributor's website. The website had been working just fine earlier in the day, but now our security system was getting in the way of the brewery undertaking its work. Upon further investigation we determined that the distributor's website had been hacked that day; hackers were attempting to use known vulnerabilities to get into visitors' computers. While our client's inability to get to their distributor's website was inconvenient, they were protected from accessing the site and so were not subject to the attempted attack. We notified the distributor of the problem. Initially they indicated that the site loaded just fine for them, and that nothing seemed wrong at their end. But after they did some more investigating, they found that while the site appeared to be operating just fine, it had in fact been hacked and was attempting to infect the computers of anyone who visited the website.

In addition to a properly secured firewall and real-time network monitoring for web traffic, it is important to keep a watchful eye on the flow of traffic in and out of your network. The two types of systems that allow this to be done are called Intrusion Detection

Systems (IDS) and Intrusion Prevention Systems (IPS). When properly set up, IDS will track, log, and notify your IT team if it detects traffic on your network that resembles an attack. The IT team can then make configuration changes and block this type of traffic. IPS, on the other hand, goes beyond detecting and notifying your IT team. When IPS is in place, it will automatically block any traffic on your network that appears to be malicious. The downside: an improperly configured IPS can block traffic that should be allowed to run in the event of a false positive. Even though it can take some tweaking to get properly configured, IPS can hugely reduce your risks. IPS and IDS are typically provided as an additional license on your firewall. When actively licensed, they receive updated security information allowing them to spot the latest threats. Again, while it would be the most secure option to set your firewall to block all traffic, that would prevent your organization from functioning. When 'holes' must be opened in your firewall, IPS and IDS can keep watch to see the type of traffic allowed through those 'holes.'

Through IDS/IPS, we continue to see attempted system attacks which are seeking out old vulnerabilities. The attackers know that many organizations do not have good patch management processes and that there are systems out there that have not been patched against these known vulnerabilities. The WannaCry ransomware, identified in 2017 and mentioned in the previous chapter, is one we continue to see attempts to exploit. It is not uncommon to see an IPS system blocking traffic identified to be an attempted WannaCry ransomware attack. The IPS system sees the traffic from an attacker and blocks their attempted attack. While the system it is trying to attack has already been updated to fix that vulnerability, this added network level security provides an additional layer in the metaphorical bullet-proof glass.

COMPUTER LEVEL PROTECTION

In addition to these layers in network protection are the layers of protection for computers themselves. These layers consist of a variety of safeguards: computer level firewalls, proper configurations, strong credentials and limited admin access, active file monitoring, and antivirus protection. Again, while there are great individual tools to help protect computers, using a multi-layered approach will greatly reduce the risk of a successful attack.

Much like your network level firewall, computers should have their own firewall enabled. All modern operating systems have built-in firewalls that can be enabled. While there are third party firewalls available, the ones built into the operating system should provide the protection you need. A third-party firewall may be useful if your IT team is unable to monitor the built-in firewalls to ensure they are properly configured. Just like monitoring your network-level firewall for changes, it is important to monitor firewall changes to individual computers and ensure you have the ability to manage them from a centralized system. Simply turning on the firewall when a computer is purchased is not enough to ensure it remains functioning and protecting the computer.

Properly configuring computers is essential in for reducing cyber risk. While a lot of attention is paid to ensuring network level configurations are managed properly, individual computer configurations are often overlooked; however, data is often breached on unprotected computers. The most common misconfigurations relate to the computer's firewall, incorrect file sharing permissions, and unnecessary remote access permissions.

I have already covered the need for proper computer level firewall monitoring, so let's take a look at file sharing and remote access configurations. One of the most common misconfigurations we run across is improper file sharing. We see this frequently with organizations that lack good vendor management. To get a piece of software to run, a vendor may want to share files from one computer to another. Due to poor change management oversight, the vendor will often share far more than what is actually needed - and with very few restrictions. It amazes me how often my team signs on a new client and discovers that all their C: drives have been shared with everyone. This means everything on the computer is shared with anyone who can communicate with it.

This is dangerous - not only could someone access information they should not, but they could also save a file onto that computer that should not be there - like a malicious program. Your IT team should not only ensure that computers are set up properly when they are deployed to users; they should also be able to monitor computers for shared data to ensure any changes that are made are done so properly.

In addition to improperly configured file sharing, we frequently run across remote access solutions that have been enabled insecurely. We typically see this - much like file shares - done by someone who needed to get a program or something working but did not fully understand what they were doing. To get it to work, the person enabled remote access to the computer without proper security precautions. Allowing remote access to a computer so that it can be controlled from somewhere else is a great tool. However, when it is used without proper security in place, this tool can provide a malicious actor full control of the computer, allowing them easy access to carry out their evil deeds. The horror!

EMPLOYEE PASSWORDS AND ADMINISTRATIVE ACCESS

Regardless of how much time and energy is spent on ensuring a computer is set up and configured properly, it can all be for nothing if weak passwords are in use and administrative access is given to users unnecessarily. We will take a deeper look at how to properly manage passwords when we look at protecting cloud services; for now, let's explore what makes for a good or bad password.

Bad passwords are all too common. I do not blame users for bad passwords, I blame the IT industry. This *XKCD* comic published in 2011 does a great job of explaining the problem and the solution:

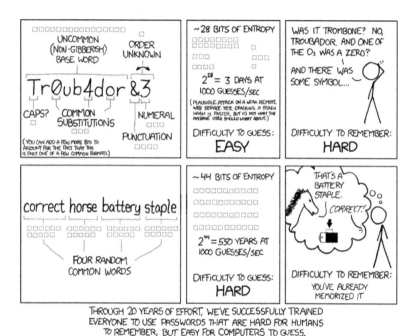

Image courtesy of xkcd.com

No matter how good a password is, there are still ways to make it a bad password. Sharing passwords is one of the easiest ways to make a good password bad. Each user should have their own unique password. Once a password is shared, it cannot be trusted to secure anything.

While certain regulatory industries still require passwords to be reset on a regular basis, this is one of the worst ways to make sure your users have good passwords. When users are forced to change their passwords regularly, they are likely to choose passwords that are simple and make changes to that password that are easy to guess. For example, if a user starts out with a password like 'Password123,' they are likely to change it to 'Password 1234' the next time they must change it. They set a bad password to start off with because they knew they would need to change it, and when it did need to be changed, the change was minor and predictable.

In addition to bad password practices, companies often give too many people administrative privileges. To make certain changes on computers, a user must have administrative privileges. I will put it bluntly: nobody should be signing into their computer with an account that has administrative privileges. When someone is actively using an account that has administrative privileges, it is way too easy for them to make a mistake, with dire consequences. However, I am not suggesting that only the IT department can make administrative changes. While this may be the most secure way to go, it frequently is not feasible. There are too many programs that require users to have administrative privileges to function; many changes that users should be able to make are prevented without these privileges.

To solve this problem, trusted users should be given access to an additional set of credentials that does have these privileges. When a change needs to be made or a program launched that requires administrative access, the user will be prompted to type in that username and password. By requiring this additional step, the user must be intentional about allowing the action; they must do more than click a button that says 'Yes.' While it is more convenient to have users sign in with an account that has administrative privileges on their computers, you are setting them and your organization up for failure.

NEXT-GEN ANTIVIRUS & SECURITY SOFTWARE

The industry still calls it Antivirus (AV) software, but the current versions of this look wildly different than what was used in the past. AV software has been used on computers since the 1980s. These AV programs would be installed on a computer, and when the company that made the AV learned about a computer virus, they would update their software with what is called a Definition. The definition would tell the AV software how to prevent the virus from taking control of the computer. This worked well; however, there was a gap between the time the problem was identified and the time the fix was in place.

Modern AV software, frequently referred to as Next-Gen AV, takes a far more advanced approach. Rather than waiting for a definition update, these programs use artificial intelligence, machine learning, and behavioral detection to identify and prevent unknown threats immediately. If your IT team is not using a next-gen AV solution, it is time to do some shopping and implement a new solution. Just like most every other item I have mentioned, AV must be properly monitored to ensure it is working effectively. Simply installing it on computers is not enough. Your IT team needs a solution that reports to a centralized location so they know that the AV is functioning properly on all computers and so they can take action if an issue is detected.

Ransomware continues to be one of the most common and destructive attacks that an organization can be hit by. While properly configured computers with active firewalls, non-administrative users and next gen AV are great for preventing these attacks, organizations need an additional, reactionary layer to stop the spread of a ransomware attack. That way, if ransomware does make it onto the computer, it is a minor inconvenience and not a door-closing event. By deploying an active file-monitoring solution with the ability to isolate a computer from a network, you can stop the spread of a ransomware attack. These attacks usually become devastating to an organization by infecting one computer and then crawling out to see what other computers are on the network that they can attack. When a file-monitoring solution is in place, files are stored on the computer that are constantly monitored for changes. These are called bait files. These bait files sit on the computer and do nothing unless something happens to them. If they are changed or modified, the computer can be set to disconnect itself immediately from the network, so the ransomware is unable to spread throughout the organization.

CLOUD SERVICES

So far, we have explored the methods to protect the technology owned and maintained by your organization. With many of the systems we rely on now moving to the 'Cloud' or being offered 'as a service,' we must extend our protection beyond the walls of our offices. While the physical infrastructure, updates and storage of these solutions usually falls to the cloud provider, your organization is still responsible for protecting your data. The most common weaknesses come through email systems, password management and user authentication.

The days of hosting your own email server should be far behind you. Companies like Microsoft and Google provide email and cloud office solutions at a scale that allows them to manage them far better than your IT team ever could, and at a fraction of the cost. While most everything is managed by Microsoft and Google, your organization must still have them set up properly. The most common misconfigurations relate to how emails are accepted by your email provider.

While I will not get into the details on configuring these, it is important to have a basic knowledge of the tools used to ensure your emails are coming from the people you think they are coming from and going to the places you want them delivered. These are called Domain Message Authentication Reporting (DMARC), Sender Policy Framework (SPF) and Domain Key Identified Mail (DKIM). SPF defines who can send emails from your domain - your domain is what comes after the @ in your email address. When this is not properly set up, someone can send an email that appears to be from someone within your organization, but actually isn't. This is called spoofing; it is used to trick an email recipient into thinking they got an email from a trusted source when it in fact came from a cybercriminal. These emails often include attachments that look legitimate but are malicious and are intended to infect the recipient's computer. DKIM makes sure the content of your email has not been tampered with or compromised from the time it leaves your inbox to when it ends up with the recipient. Without DKIM, it is possible for your email to be intercepted and modified to include malicious content before it gets to the recipient. DMARC ties SPF and DKIM together to ensure an added layer of security.

Phishing, a scam where criminals impersonate legitimate organizations in an email to try and trick you into providing them information, continues to be one of the leading causes of data breaches. We will discuss methods in the next chapter for helping your users avoid falling for these scams; for now, know that a technical solution to help prevent these messages from ever getting to your users is a must. Enabling the previously mentioned settings will help avoid receiving phishing messages, but they alone are not enough. A proper filtering solution for email should be put in place.

Filtering solutions come in different forms. Some are available directly from your email provider, like Microsoft or Google, while others are provided by third parties. They all work similarly, though. Incoming email messages are sent through filters before they can be delivered to your inbox. Like modern AV, filtering solutions often make use of AI and machine learning to help prevent the delivery of malicious emails. In addition to these advanced features, basic filters should be set up to examine each aspect of an email, such as the sender's name in relation to the emails you normally receive from them. While these do require some tweaking, and trial and error, they are an absolute necessity to help reduce the risk of a cyber incident.

As previously discussed, passwords continue to be a thorn in the paw of every computer user. We have conditioned people to use bad passwords, leaving them at great risk of having their accounts breached. While there is a large effort under way to develop passwordless access methods, passwords remain a part of our everyday lives; so, it isn't enough to just ask users to have better password hygiene. We need to provide solutions for our users to set up robust and secure passwords.

By using a password management system within your organization, you can greatly reduce your chances of a breach due to bad passwords. A good password management system allows your users to store their individual passwords in a secure location that they can access whenever and wherever they need. They provide a method for sharing passwords securely for those websites and services that do not allow for unique usernames and passwords for each of your users. Password managers should also be capable of running on a user's computer so that it will put the username and password into the login fields for the user when they access the website or service.

In addition to these features, you must have the ability to audit your password management system. Your password management system should have:

» the ability to see the overall strength of your users' passwords
» the age of those passwords
» a way for management to identify which shared passwords a user has accessed in the past

When an employee leaves an organization, there is often a rush to figure out the parameters of what they had access to. Were they the ones that set up the company's Instagram account? Did they know the password to the company's website? The list can be huge!

We all know that we need to change certain passwords when a user leaves our organization. The problem is that organizations frequently do not have any idea which passwords the departed employee knew, or even set up and was the only person who knew that password – social media managers are often in this position. The option at that point is to change every shared password or to dig a hole, bury our heads in it, and hope the former employee does not do something bad. With a lost password, regaining access to, for example, an organization's Twitter account can become a nightmare.

There is a better way. A well-designed password management system will allow you to run a report to see which passwords the employee had stored in their individual password vault as well as any shared passwords they accessed. Having this information readily at hand will easily allow you to change the few passwords the employee would have known and to see what services need to be transferred to another employee.

In addition to easy and secure storage of passwords and auditing, the password management system can be set to require passwords of a certain length and complexity. While the *XKCD* comic above provides a great way to create secure passwords that are easy to remember, a good password management system should allow your users to create strong passwords that do not need to be remembered. These are called 'Copy/Paste' passwords. They are long and complex. Someone could see it and have little to no chance of being able to remember it. Here's an example: ZIP8b6Xa(^!St5OaM84. If you asked your employees to try and remember a password like that, they would probably get up and walk out the door (I would!). But if that password is stored in a password manager that can drop the password in for your user, the employees do not ever need to know what the actual password is, let alone try and remember it.

No matter how good your passwords are, every online system should be set up to use Multi-Factor Authentication (MFA). The theory behind MFA is that not only should a user need to provide something they know (their username and password) but that they should also be required to provide something that only they have access to, for example, a code from an app on their phone. Highly secure systems go one step further, by requiring users to provide a third factor, like a fingerprint or iris scan. While your organization may not need to scan your employees' eyeballs before they can access their email, you absolutely need to have employees provide some sort of secondary authentication, like a code from an app on their phone. These typically come from an app called an authenticator. Once set up, the app will provide a unique six-digit number for each online account, that refreshes every 30 seconds. During the sign-in process, the user enters in their username and password and is then prompted to enter in this code. According to Microsoft, users with MFA will end up blocking an astonishing 99.9% of automated attacks. With data breaches being so common - and MFA being so effective - MFA is absolutely one of the most important things you can do to protect your organization.

While these technical solutions need to be in place, social engineering, or the process of tricking people into providing access to systems, remains one of the leading causes of data breaches. In the next chapter we will explore the non-technical solutions by which you can educate your employees and put policies in place to protect your organization against a cyberattack.

CHAPTER SUMMARY

» There are many aspects to securing your computers and data. Several of these are technical in nature.

» No one solution can be relied on to protect your organization.

» Security solutions need to be layered on top of one another like the materials used in bullet proof glass. While a malicious attack may get through one or two layers, there need to be many other layers in place so that it can be caught and stopped before it causes problems.

» These solutions need to be implemented at the network level, computer level and for your cloud services. Network level solutions will help prevent the flow of malicious traffic between your computers. Computer level protection will help to stop problems that get through the network level protection so it cannot cause any actual harm to your computers and data.

» Cloud services may be provided and managed by a third party, but it is your responsibility to protect your data. The most common threat to cloud systems is unauthorized access.

» By having a password manager in place, you can help your employees to create strong passwords as well as generate reports that will help you identify what an employee had access to when their employment ends.

» Multi Factor Authentication (MFA) provides an additional layer of protection beyond a username and password. A user is required to enter in a code that is provided to them when they want to log in. MFA is one of the most effective methods to protect against unauthorized access to cloud systems.

» Your IT team should be implementing the technical solutions as well as monitoring them to ensure they are working properly.

Chapter 8:

SECURITY – OPERATIONAL SOLUTIONS

The technical solutions we looked at in the previous chapter have been developed to prevent security incidents - and they have done an amazing job. But while these tech solutions must be in place, they simply are not enough. Because these solutions have gotten so good, attackers have had to adapt to remain successful. In Kevin D. Mitnick's *Ghost in the Wires: My Adventure as the World's Most Wanted Hacker*, he provides insight into how cybercriminals are able to bypass technical safeguards through social engineering: "the casual or calculated manipulation of people to influence them to do things they would not ordinarily do. And convincing them without raising the least hint of suspicion. Through social engineering, criminals can bypass the technical safeguards when they trick an employee into handing them the keys to the castle."

According to the IMB Cyber Security Intelligence Index Report, "Human error was a major contributing cause in 95% of all breaches." While there are still many opportunities for technical hacking, malicious actors have found that phishing and social engineering are incredibly effective ways to breach organizations. These attempts have skyrocketed due to their effectiveness and can cause significant damage to an organization. Employees are hired because of their ability to perform the tasks needed by the organization. We need them to get their jobs done and often do not want to take away from the time they need to do their jobs. But the more we learn about how modern data breaches happen, we fear a mistake an employee makes could cause major issues for our organizations. Just like we wish the bad guys would leave our computers alone, we wish they would leave our employees alone, too. Employees should not be burdened by the idea that they could make a mistake that causes the entire operation to close down. Unfortunately, that is the world we live in. It is our responsibility to provide our employees with the tools they need to be successful.

We simply cannot trust our technical safeguards alone to protect us from cyber threats. We must empower our employees to do their part. This should be done through two avenues: policies and education.

POLICIES

I frequently talk to business managers and owners who say things like, "Our employees know better than to do XYZ on their work computers. They are a good group of people." The reality is that people will take the shortest path to accomplish the task at hand. When we do not inform employees of the way things should and should not be done, we leave them without the tools they need. When you as the leader create clear policies, your employees will have a clear understanding of what can and cannot be done with your organization's computers and data. There will be little to no debate about what is and is not acceptable. While we may have amazing employees, they cannot read our minds. Likewise, while we may think we know what we expect, we do not even know our *own* expectations of employees - until we have them down on paper.

This blind spot can be overcome by developing a set of policies for your organization. The following policies should be in place:

» **Computer Use.** This policy will detail what is and is not allowed to be done on work computers. This standard is not only important for employees in the office, but for employees working remotely as well. While you may have purchased a nice laptop for your employee to work from home, they may view it as an opportunity to have a new family computer on which the kids can complete their schoolwork. Before you know it, that computer is full of junk from the games the kids were playing instead of doing their homework. By setting clear expectations, employees know what is and is not acceptable as parameters for use of their work computers.

» **Network Security.** Informing your employees of the technical and physical safeguards that are in place empowers them. They should be aware of security protocols, so they do not attempt to bypass them. If there is a security problem, your employees should know how their computer will behave and what to look out for.

» **Access Control.** Technical configurations should be in place to restrict who can access certain data within your organization. This may come in the form of file share access restrictions, but these systems can and often do suffer from the occasional misconfiguration or misuse. Make it clear to employees that they are not to access certain types of information and that tracking systems may be in place to see who has accessed certain data; this can help ensure that employees do the right thing even if they do come across data which they should not be able to access.

» **BYOD Policy.** A lot of companies have adopted a Bring Your Own Device (BYOD) strategy. In terms of maintaining data security, I am strongly against allowing employees to use their personal devices for work purposes. That being said, there are certain times when it does make sense to allow an employee to use their personal devices; having a clear policy that requires them to register the devices with the organization and maintain a certain level of security is a must.

» **Disposal Procedure.** Defining how old devices can be disposed of is important from both an environmental and a data security perspective. Electronic waste represents 2% of America's trash in landfills, but it represents 70% of overall toxic waste. As the owner of the equipment, you have both the legal and ethical responsibility to ensure that it does not cause a negative environmental impact. In addition to our responsibility to Mother Earth is our responsibility to properly protect our organizations' data. Ensure that computers storing company data do not end up in the hands of someone who could use it maliciously.

» **Termination & Sanction Policy.** Define what happens to an employee's access when their position with the organization has ended. While a technical procedure to remove access needs to be defined and followed, it is important to state clearly what is and is not allowed after employment has been terminated. Define the repercussions of violating these policies. When the consequences are clearly defined, employees know what will happen.

It is not good enough to just have these policies in a book somewhere. They must be provided to employees, and employees must acknowledge that they understand and agree to abide by them. By having a firm understanding of what is and is not allowed, along with the consequences of violating the policies, employees are far more likely to avoid behavior that will cause your organization problems.

POLICIES CHECKLIST

Here is a checklist of the policies I have itemized above. As a quick sense-check as to where your organization is right now, tick each one of these six which you know you have in place.

1. **Computer use policy**
2. **Network security policy**
3. **Access control policy**
4. **BYOD policy**
5. **Disposal procedure policy**
6. **Termination & sanction policy**

Have you been able to tick them all? If not, plug the gaps by drawing up and implementing appropriate policies.

TRAINING

With social engineering being one of the leading causes of data breaches, it is our responsibility to empower our employees to defend themselves against such attacks. By developing a cyber security training program for your organization, you can turn your weaknesses into your strongest defense. There are many programs available to implement, without having to build your own. It is important to not only have one of these programs, but to ensure it is in place and being used. At minimum, cyber security training should be completed as part of a new employee's onboarding process and be completed again annually. When your employees complete their training annually, they are receiving updated information on modern threats and can keep cyber security top of mind.

A well-rounded training program should include:

» **Type of Information.** You should clearly define the type of information your organization stores and how each different type of information can cause problems for the organization if it falls into the wrong hands. This can range from employee records containing Personally Identifiable Information (PII) to information covered under the Health Insurance Portability and Accountability Act (HIPAA), and include financial information such as credit card numbers. Each type of information can cause major trouble for both the employee and the organization if it is not properly protected.

» **Presentation of Threats.** Your employees should be given clear examples of how threats to your organization can present themselves, such as phishing emails, social engineering phone calls and websites with misleading pop-ups. By understanding what these threats look like and how they are presented, employees can more easily spot them.

» **Phishing Identification.** While general threat presentation is good to understand, phishing scams continue to be a main tool of social engineering. There are several specific items employees should be trained to look for in an email to determine if it is safe or not.

» **Phone Scam Identification.** Most users probably know how to avoid a car warranty scam call, but phone scams that are not as obvious are frequently used towards organizations in targeted attacks. Training employees on how to spot these and to verify a caller's identity will go a long way.

» **Password Security.** Users should be provided the tools and information about how to correctly use, store and create passwords.

» **Wi-Fi Connections.** It has become relatively common knowledge that not all Wi-Fi is secure, but employees need to be educated on how to identify a trustworthy connection and what to do when they access Wi-Fi networks that do not belong to your organization.

» **Physical Device Protection.** Employees take laptops to meetings and home to work remotely. It is important they understand how to secure their devices both in the office and while transporting them.

» **Use of Personal Devices.** Employees need to understand the risks of using personal devices for work purposes. While it may be convenient, there are risks to your organization's data and security involved that they must understand.

» **Employment Repercussions.** Employees need to understand that cybersecurity is not just the responsibility of the IT department. While there are certain protections against individual liability, your employees need to understand that they have a responsibility to do their part in preventing cyber incidents, and that there may be employment consequences if they fail to do so.

» **Incident Management & Reporting.** If an incident does happen, employees need to know how to handle and report the issue.

Like security policies, simply offering a training solution is not enough. You need accountability to track who has completed the training and that they are able to demonstrate their understanding of the information. Training must be completed at least annually; however, I highly recommend offering more frequent, mini trainings throughout the year to keep employees up to speed with modern trends and to keep cybersecurity top of mind.

Go to www.speakingtheirlanguage.com/freetraining and I will set up your organization on our training platform for free.

Once security policies and a training program have been implemented, additional tools can be used to check how well your employees do at spotting and detecting threats. One of the most beneficial tools comes in the form of a **phishing test**. Users within your organization are sent an email that is safe but mimics a real-life phishing attack. It will track to determine who, if anyone, falls for the attack. We frequently see a great response from users who have gone through security training; they are able to put their skills to use and determine the email is a scam. While most users who have been trained properly are able to spot these phishing tests and report them, we do still see some users who fall for them. These are typically users who have not completed the training or who did not take it seriously. Once the user has fallen for the scam and finds out that it was in fact a simulation, they usually take the information more seriously. After the scare, these users become effective at spotting and combating phishing against themselves and your organization.

Through a multi-layered approach of both technical and operational security measures, your organization will be in a good position to reduce the risk of a cyber-attack. While there is no way to prevent every potential incident 100% of the time, these systems must be implemented to give your organization a fighting chance. It is rare for us to run across a potential client who has these safeguards in place and has experienced a breach. It is, however, extremely common for us to talk with organizations who did not have these in place and have experienced a breach. By the time we are talking with the organization, they have suffered the loss of critical data, been unable to serve their clients, and experienced both a reputation and financial loss. The tools exist to prevent this from happening and must be implemented to keep your organization from becoming a negative cyber security statistic.

SAFEGUARDS CHECKLIST

Here is a checklist of the safeguards I have itemized above. As a quick sense-check as to where your organization is right now, tick each one of these eleven you know you have in place.

1. **Clear definitions of types of information stored**
2. **Presentation of threats to employees**
3. **Phishing scam identification training**
4. **Phishing scam simulation tests**
5. **Phone scam identification**
6. **Password security training**
7. **Wi-Fi connection trustworthiness training**
8. **Physical device protection**
9. **Clear policy on use of personal devices**
10. **Awareness of employment repercussions**
11. **Incident management & reporting in place**

Have you been able to tick them all? If not, plug the gaps with appropriate training and policies.

While these tools do an amazing job at preventing problems, there is always a chance that problems will occur. In the next chapter, we will explore the backup and recovery systems that must be in place to allow you to return to normal operations in the event of a cyber incident, natural disaster, or hardware failure.

CHAPTER SUMMARY

» Technical cybersecurity solutions are not enough to protect your organization.

» Employees need to be educated on the role they play in keeping your systems and data secure.

» There are two operational solutions that must be in place: policies and training. Your organization should have a clearly defined set of policies for what employees are and are not allowed to do with your computers and data. These policies cannot simply exist in a binder on a shelf. They must be reviewed by employees annually and they must sign off that they have reviewed and agree to abide by them.

» A cybersecurity training program must also be in place. Employees should be educated on how modern threats present themselves, so they know what to look out for. They need to understand the repercussions both to them individually and to your organization if a cyber-event does occur. They should be trained at least annually, but more frequently is better.

Chapter 9:

BUSINESS CONTINUITY & DISASTER RECOVERY

By implementing the technical and policy-based solutions discussed in previous chapters, organizations are far less likely to experience a disaster. However, anyone that guarantees you that nothing bad can happen is full of it. The SolarWinds hack discovered in December 2020, which saw government agencies such as the US Treasury and Commerce Department as well as private companies like Microsoft and Cisco breached, taught us that no one is impenetrable from cyber-attacks. The Tokyo Stock Exchange shutdown on October 1, 2020, showed us that systems can fail, and poorly tested recovery procedures can result in outages with significant impacts.

When we accept that large organizations can suffer from these incidents and that small and medium-size businesses are as much of a target for cybercriminals, we know that disaster can strike anyone. When disaster happens, we are unable to serve our clients and provide them the products and services they depend on us for. Employees are still getting paid while they are unable to perform their duties. The ability to bring money in the door stops. Knowing that these things can happen instills fear and anxiety. Leaving your organization's future up to 'good fortune' is too risky. Your organization has too many good things to offer to let a technical disaster force you out of business.

The final layer of protection for your organization's protection is a well-developed Business Continuity and Disaster Recovery (BCDR) plan. These plans allow your organization to continue to operate and maintain continuity during a disaster and recover when a disaster does occur. A good BCDR strategy requires proper planning and technical components. In this chapter, we will look at how to protect your organization, beginning with the planning phase. We will also take a high-level look at the technical solutions and implementation of a well-developed BCDR strategy.

PLANNING FOR A DISASTER

Organizations must have a well-defined disaster recovery plan. These plans are living documents that cannot simply be written up and put on a shelf. They must be reviewed regularly, kept up to date and key players must know their roles in the process. The key components of a good disaster recovery plan are:

» **Plan Updating.** This section will define the process for reviewing and updating the plan. Saying that a plan will be reviewed and updated is not enough. The plan itself must define what will be done at this level and when.

» **Plan Storage.** Your plan will be your guidebook during a disaster. It is critical that your team knows where it will be kept ensuring it is accessible in the event of a disaster.

» **Backup Strategy.** The methods by which you will back up your systems and data need to be clearly defined. This will include information about the types of backups you are using and details about how each individual system within your critical infrastructure is backed up.

» **Risk Management.** You must determine the types of disasters that may impact your organization and how they may impact you. This will differ based on both the way you operate and your geographical location. For example: some organizations may have a high risk of floods, while others are more susceptible to forest fires. Know the risks where you are and plan appropriately.

» **Emergency Response.** When disaster strikes, you should already know who will be responding and in what capacity. Responder responsibilities should include everything from client notifications to the technical side of recovering data.

» **Media Contact.** You must define who will be responsible for responding to media inquiries and how they will respond. Your organization's reputation may be on the line during a disaster, so it is important to ensure these communications are handled properly.

» **Insurance.** Your organization must make sure it is properly insured and that the relevant people know how to engage the appropriate insurance agencies when a disaster strikes.

» **System Recovery Plan.** This section will be technical, and much like the rollback strategy in the change management process detailed in Chapter 4, will provide clear guidance on the recovery process to follow. This will prove to be critical when people are stressed and tensions are high.

» **DRP Exercises.** A well-defined plan for testing and practicing the Disaster Recovery Process should be in place. It should not only define the process you will run to confirm your plan will work, but the frequency of performing these exercises and a logbook to confirm they have been done.

Go to www.speakingtheirlanguage.com/drp for a free Disaster Recovery Template you can take and modify for your organization.

DISASTER RECOVERY PLAN CHECKLIST

As with the safeguards in the previous chapter, check to see how prepared your organization is. Answer YES/NO truthfully to each question, to check that you know what is in place and operating effectively. Any marked 'No', or you are not sure about, act now to fix them!

» Are updates of our plan in place and documented?
YES ___ NO ___

» Does our team know where our DRP is stored?
YES___ NO___

» Do we have a clear backup strategy?
YES___ NO___

» Have we conducted a clear risk management assessment?
YES___ NO___

» Do we know who will undertake any emergency response?
YES___ NO___

» Is our media contact known and trained?
YES___ NO___

» Is our insurance in place and our insurance contact known by relevant team members?
YES___ NO___

» Is there a systems recovery plan in place?
YES___ NO___

» Is a plan for testing and practicing our DRP in place?
YES___ NO___

BACKUP & RECOVERY

There are three categories I use to classify disasters that need to be accounted for to restore your organization's data and ability to operate: interruption, data corruption, and destruction.

Interruptions

Interruptions can be as simple as a user error that causes lost time or productivity. A solution should be in place to allow the employee to get back to work quickly, without having to recreate the work they have already done. These types of backups should be able to resolve a problem where a file has been deleted that should not have been, or modifications to a file have been mistakenly made that would be time-consuming to correct. These situations can be resolved by having file-level backup in place.

This type of backup will take the files on a user's computer or in a shared drive and back them up frequently with revision history or versioning. Revision history or versioning allows for a single file to be backed up with the ability to return that file to where it was at a specific point in time. Rather than overwriting the backed-up file with the current version each time the file is changed, all versions are kept as changes are made. This allows for a user to recover a file from a time before a major change was made that caused a problem.

We frequently see this needed in situations where a file such as a complex spreadsheet is shared with multiple users who make regular changes to the data. It is not uncommon for a user to mistakenly change a portion of that spreadsheet that they should not have altered. While they may not have the information needed to fix the data another user is responsible for, a file level backup allows the spreadsheet to be restored to the way it was before they made the error.

File level backups are frequently cloud-based solutions but may be a hybrid solution with backup copies kept on-site. Because the amount of data that needs to be uploaded to the backup server is minimal, the data can be backed up over the internet quickly. If internet reliability or speed is a problem, it may make sense to use a hybrid solution where data is backed up both to an on-site location and to the cloud. When data needs to be recovered, a user can quickly find the proper version of the file that needs to be restored and download it to the computer.

When deciding if the backups should be saved on-site or only in the cloud, I recommend determining the amount of time it would take to restore any given file at any given point. If the files are small like Word documents, and they can be restored within a few seconds, you may not need to keep a backed-up copy on-site since the files can be restored through the internet so quickly. If the files are large, like videos, it may take a longer time for the backups to be completed and for them to be restored from a cloud-based backup solution. In this case, it makes sense to keep an on-site backup copy in addition to the copy stored in the cloud.

When determining your backup method, have a solution in place that will allow the file to be restored faster than the employee could recreate the data. Determine if the computer being backed up will always be in the office, or if it is a laptop that travels with remote workers. If the laptop is frequently out of office, relying on a backup solution that only functions while the computer is in the office would leave the data at risk when the employee is off-site.

Data Corruption
Data corruption takes place when an individual system fails due to a software or hardware malfunction. While file-level backup is in place and will allow the user to get their work back, their computer may need to be rebuilt or replaced. Some computers may be quick and easy to rebuild or replace for a user; however, many have complex software installations and customized configurations that may not be able to be backed up using a file-level backup system. In this case, a system-level backup should be in place.

A system-level backup will allow your IT team to restore an entire computer back to where it was prior to the problem. System-level backups are more complex, store significantly more data than file-level backups and take longer to back up and to restore. Determine where these types of backups will be deployed by determining the time it will take to restore the backup in relation to the time it would take to set the user up with a new computer or a fresh installation. If the user primarily uses email, document, and web-based software, it may be faster to simply set up a spare computer for the user; then, restore their files from a file-level backup. In this scenario you would not have to wait for an entire system-level backup for restoration.

In other cases, users may run software that takes a large amount of time to install and configure before the user can be operational again. A system-level backup can save a lot of time and reduce lost productivity. Due to the size of these files, these backups are typically saved to a backup system that is stored on-site. The local computer network can save a system copy in its current state in a matter of minutes; a cloud-based system may take hours to complete the backup. To provide an additional level of protection, these systems frequently have what is called "cloud replication". Instead of the computer backing up directly to a cloud location, the system backs up to an on-site location which then replicates that data to the cloud. When these types of restores are needed, they can usually be completed by using the on-site backup system. This allows for a fast restore from a very recent backup job.

Hardware/software Destruction
Destruction is what most users think of when they hear disaster recovery. Think of the cleanup that happens after tornadoes, fires, floods, burst pipes, or any other event that destroys hardware. To protect against data and productivity losses due to these types of problems, system level backups should be in place that have enhanced abilities to restore quickly. These backups must be saved both on-site and to a cloud backup solution.

All servers and critical computers within an organization should have this type of backup in place, but the extent of the solution will vary. Determining the extent to which these backup systems are implemented should be based strictly on the cost of downtime. If a particular system fails or is destroyed by a natural disaster but does not cost the company any money while it is down, it will not make sense to have a highly sophisticated backup solution for that system. On the other hand, if a single system fails and your entire organization cannot function properly until it is operational again, you would be wise to invest in a full BCDR backup solution.

To determine your BCDR backup plan, examine both the lost expenses you will incur after a disaster, as well as the lost revenue. Determining your potential lost expenses can be done by using this formula: Loss = H(P/2080). H is the amount of time a system is down, in hours. P is the total annual payroll cost, including benefits, taxes, and wages of the employees who are unable to function while the system is down. The number 2,080 accounts for the hourly cost assuming employees work 40 hours per week for 52 weeks each year. For example: if a department has $750,000 worth of annual payroll, and a system is down for 32 working hours, the formula would be Loss = 32($750,000/2080). In this case, the downtime due to a disaster would cost the organization $11,538.

To determine lost revenue, the formula Loss = H(G/T) is used. H is the amount of time that a system is down in hours. G is the gross annual revenue, and T is the total annual operating hours. For example: if a system is down for 32 hours, the company has a gross revenue of $3M and operates for a total of 2,080 hours each year (again assuming 40 hours each week for 52 weeks), the formula would be Loss = 32($3M/2080). In this case, the lost revenue would be $46,254. When accounting for the lost expenses and lost revenue in this example, a 32-hour downtime would cost $57,692.

Once you determine your company's numbers, calculate the value of a full BCDR solution to determine if the cost makes sense. These solutions are relatively expensive due to their complexity. They typically involve a local backup of the critical systems to an on-site appliance that is not only capable of storing all the data, but also of booting the backed-up systems as virtual machines so they can be up and running within a short period of time. A virtual machine is just like a physical computer or server, except the physical hardware is mimicked on what is referred to as a host; the host can run multiple virtualized systems at any given time. The virtual machine operates just like the physical system did but runs on the local appliance until the affected computer can be restored, repaired, or replaced.

BCDR solutions back up to a cloud location in addition to the local appliance. The cloud location, like the on-site appliance, not only stores the data; it can also boot up the systems off-site so they can be accessed remotely, as if they were running within an office. While it is important that these systems allow for the environment to be able to run on a local or cloud appliance so the organization can resume operations, they also must be able to be restored to new hardware once the disaster has been mitigated and the office or hardware is physically reassembled.

Each of these solutions should be able to withstand user errors or physical damage, but they also need to be able to function in the event of a cyber-attack. If your solutions are set up in a way that makes them vulnerable to an attack, they will not help your organization recover from a disaster. To accommodate this, these solutions must be run independently and isolated from your production environment. Isolating backup infrastructure from your other systems means having it on independent hardware that is independently accessible and managed from your other computers and servers. If your backups are stored on your production servers or integrated with them in a way that would give an attacker access, they cannot be trusted as a reliable recovery method.

PUTTING IT ALL TOGETHER

Having a well thought out and developed BCDR strategy means having the correct backup systems in place as well as having a plan for what to do in the event of a disaster. Both the technical and operational systems should be tested regularly so you can confidently rely on them when needed. Go through these exercises with the recovery team and determine if the solution actually works; tweak the plan as the needs of your organization evolve.

By having technical security solutions, operational security solutions, and a BCDR strategy in place, your organization will have the necessary layers in place to prevent an incident from occurring. If an incident does occur, your organization can recover.

CHAPTER SUMMARY

» Implementing technical and operation security solutions will greatly reduce the likelihood of an event that causes downtime or lost data.

» However, cyber-attacks, hardware failures and natural disasters can still occur, no matter how well protected you are against them.

» Your organization needs a solution in place to be able to recover quick in the event of a disaster. This starts by having a well-defined Disaster Recovery Plan (DRP). The plan will allow your team to take actions that have been well throughout and planned for ahead of time when a disaster occurs. The plan will include the technical methods that are used for data backup.

» Backup solutions vary greatly in abilities and cost. The extent of your backup solution should directly relate to the cost of being down or losing data.

» While full blown business continuity and disaster recovery solutions can be very expensive, the cost can be well worth it if your organization would lose a substantial amount of money due to a disaster. This is the final layer in a multi-layered solution to protect your organization. It must be well thought out and actively maintained to ensure it will function properly when needed.

Chapter 10:

REMOTE WORKFORCE

Allowing employees to work outside of the main office is nothing new. Branch offices are commonplace and work from home positions have been available for quite some time. In March of 2020, the world was turned upside down by the Covid-19 pandemic. Restrictions were put in place preventing employees from going into work; many organizations were not prepared for functioning without their staff working within their four walls. To stay in business, employers were forced to change the way they operated, virtually overnight. So, in many cases, these changes were made rapidly, with minimal thought given to the security vulnerabilities that come into play when employees work outside of the office. Great solutions have been available for quite some time, and it was so unfortunate to see so many organizations scramble and create security problems while making this transition.

Whether you allow employees to work remotely as a perk or as a strategic benefit, or you are forced to accommodate this due to a global pandemic, it is important to have a solution in place that allows for maximum productivity without jeopardizing security.

In terms of productivity and efficiency, look at how your overall systems are set up. Relying on systems that are hosted within the walls of your office can reduce the ability for your employees to be efficient while working remotely. With so many solutions being cloud-based and provided as a service, review your methods and solutions, with the ability to work remotely in mind. These systems often present an opportunity for long-term cost savings, in addition to easy and secure remote access.

As we discussed in Chapter 1, email systems are a great example of this. It used to make sense to run your own email server; now it can be run in a cloud environment at a greatly reduced cost, with easier and more secure access for remote users. Many types of business applications, the programs you run that are specific to your industry, are created by organizations that are only a fraction of the size of Microsoft and Google. Now that cloud infrastructure is much more accessible and less expensive for these vendors to obtain and manage, they are quickly adapting the Software as a Service model. Take the time to check with your vendors to see what they are able to offer in terms of hosted options. By having a vendor host and maintain the servers that allow their program to run, you will likely see a long-term cost savings, and you will usually find that they are much better suited for remote access since the program is no longer confined to your company network.

When looking at cost savings, it is important to not only look at the annual licensing and maintenance costs, but also at the costs of purchasing, owning, and maintaining your own infrastructure. While the pricing may not look comparable at first, it usually balances out when all aspects are considered. Even if a hosted solution costs more, the benefits it may provide in terms of remote accessibility may be well worth the cost. In addition to your unique line of business systems, explore modern tools for communication and collaboration that have been developed to meet the needs of a remote workforce. Tools like video conferencing and internal messaging have come a long way and may not only improve the ability for employees to work remotely, but also the way your team operates within the office. The range and availability of these types of remote-working tools has expanded greatly following the effects of Covid-19.

One of the most common modern dilemmas we all face is that of security and privacy versus convenience. Over the last decade we have seen a massive shift in what people are willing to give up in terms of privacy to make their lives more convenient. I cannot imagine the look on my grandfather's face if I would have brought an Amazon Alexa into his house twenty years ago. While he may have been blown away by its abilities, I am willing to bet he would have thrown it out the door when I told him that everything he said around it would be provided to and stored by strangers who would use that information to manipulate his buying habits. Today, nearly 90 million adults within the US own a smart speaker. These are your employees; you can bet they are going to find the most convenient and efficient way to get their work done, even if it means operating in a way that is less secure. It is our job as managers to ensure we have convenient systems in place that also meet the security needs of our organizations.

It all comes down to access. The easier we make it for employees to access the systems and data they need to do their jobs, the more efficient they can be while working remotely. Making these systems and data easy to access does not mean having to create security holes, though. The two questions that must be answered are *how will employees access the needed material* and *where from?*

HOW DO EMPLOYEES REMOTELY ACCESS COMPANY RESOURCES?

If the solutions your organization uses are entirely cloud-based, then you have an easy answer to this question. Your employees can gain access to these solutions remotely, just like they would from the office. The question becomes more difficult when there are resources within your physical office that employees need to be able to function. One of the most common mistakes organizations make when setting employees up to work remotely is opening up their local resources to the world so employees have access. This is not just a mistake: to my mind, it is blatantly stupid.

Someone from the company will create an exception to the firewall rule to allow access to a resource on the network from anywhere on the internet. For example: consider the back-end database for software that runs on a server within your office. While it is normally only accessible while in the office, someone allows the database to be accessed over the internet so the software on the employee's computer can run from anywhere in the world. While this is incredibly convenient for the employee, it creates a gaping security hole and vulnerability for your organization. It is not only incredibly easy for your employee to get access to it when done this way – it is easy for an attacker to gain access too. Remember those ransomware hazards!

Here is another example, one we saw many misguided organizations undertake when the Covid-19 pandemic forced employees to work remotely: enabling Windows Remote Desktop (RDP) over the internet. Enabling this has allowed employees to connect to their work computers quickly and easily from anywhere in the world. They might be on a personal computer at their kitchen table, but they were able to connect to their office computer and work just like they were sitting at their desk. Again, this was very convenient for the employee, but also very convenient for cybercriminals. Instead of a criminal having to break into your office, sit down at an employee's computer and start guessing passwords, they could do it from the comfort of their homes. Attackers use automated systems that try a combination of common usernames and passwords, or ones that have been found in data breaches, to attempt to log into your computers. They are incredibly good at this. This is called a brute force attack;

as the name suggests, attackers throw a ton of usernames and passwords at a computer until they find one that works. Once the attacker has access to the computer, they, like your employees, can do whatever they want remotely.

In addition to brute force attacks, there have been known vulnerabilities that can allow an attacker to bypass even having to provide an accurate username and password to gain access to the computer. While patches have been released to fix the known vulnerabilities for RDP, many organizations have not installed these patches, and so new vulnerabilities continue to be found. For employees to access the resources within your office, a secure remote access system must be put in place. This can come in the form of a Virtual Private Network (VPN), or through one of the many alternatives to RDP that can be set up to provide access without having to open up your computers for the world to see. A VPN allows a remote computer to connect securely to the office network. Once it is connected, the computer operates just like it does when it is in the office. This can be very convenient when your employees run software on their computers that rely on resources from a company server. Using an RDP alternative is a great solution as well. It allows your employees to take control of the computer at their desk and operate just like they are sitting in the office. This is great for employees who are needing to temporarily work remotely, or who do so only on occasion. It is not always suitable for employees who work remotely full time because it does require a dedicated computer to be set up and running in the office.

WHERE DO THEY NEED ACCESS FROM?

Whether an employee is using a VPN or an RDP alternative to work remotely, they need a computer. Another common security issue that many organizations created for themselves during the onset of the pandemic was allowing employees to use personal computers to work remotely. While the need to adapt quickly may have justified this in the short term, there are many organizations continuing this practice today. The bottom line is: **employees should not use personal computers for work purposes**. Your organization has no ability to manage these devices to ensure they are properly patched and secured. In addition to the cybersecurity concerns, you lose control over your data. Once it has been stored on a personal computer, you do not have the ability to remove that data. If an employee leaves the organization, that data may very well leave with them too. This data may contain client information or priority data. It is simply irresponsible to allow this type of data to be left outside of your organization's control.

Allowing employees to use personal computers to connect remotely via VPN can be even more dangerous. While they may only be using their personal computer to connect remotely to their office computer, their personal laptop is now on the company network. If the computer has been compromised, it can begin attempting to compromise other computers and servers within your office. You should not allow employees to connect via a VPN using their personal computers for the same reason that you would not allow them to bring the personal computer into the office and plug them into your organization's network.

An exception can be made for the use of personal computers if a proper RDP alternative is in use. By using a secure remote access system that does not actually place the personal computer on your company network, like a Virtual Private Network would, employees can control their work computers while keeping their personal computer isolated from other company systems. There are many great solutions available that can provide a relatively secure method for your employees to work remotely without having to send them home with a company-owned device. However, the best solution is to always have employees using computers that are owned by your organization. This can be cost-prohibitive for organizations but is without a doubt the only way you can ensure you have control over access to your systems and data.

Working remotely is here to stay. Many organizations previously had the mindset that they would never be able to function outside of their office. Being forced to work remotely taught them that this simply is not true. Having and maintaining an office is frequently the largest expense for an organization, behind payroll. The pandemic has shown many organizations that they can operate without an office, or with a much smaller office than they had before. Whether you are closing your physical location and moving to a remote workforce or simply allowing some employees to work from home as a perk, the days of having everyone working within an office are behind us. Taking advantage of modern tools that allow for efficient work outside of your office is a must. Ensuring your organization's remote employees are not only efficient but are also secure is essential to keeping your doors open. Having your employees work outside of your office does not mean that your systems and data must live in the wild wild west. There are incredibly powerful and effective tools that can provide both efficiency and security. It is critical to ensure they are in place.

CHAPTER SUMMARY

» Remote working is here to stay. It may be a temporary solution to accommodate employee needs or a long-term solution that provides a strategic benefit to your organization. Either way, remote employees must be set up to work in a way that promotes productivity without jeopardizing security.

» The easier you make it for them to operate securely, the more likely they will. When moving to a remote workforce, review how employees will access company resources and where they will access them from.

» If your company resources are primarily cloud-based, then secure remote access should already be in place. If the data resides within your office, then a plan needs to be made to provide access securely.

» Outside of some limited circumstances, avoid having employees us personal devices for remote work. Provide them the correct computer equipment so they can be productive, and you can stay in control of your data.

Chapter 11:

TECHNICAL SUPPORT

Many IT companies have done a disservice to their clients by offering hourly technical support as their main and central service. While everyone needs to have a good technical support team on their side, there is so much more to IT than having someone to help you when stuff breaks. As we have explored the areas that are critical to a successful IT strategy in the previous chapters, you have gotten a glimpse into the myriad of systems and solutions at play. These systems can have a profound impact on protecting your organization and ensuring a productive workforce, but they cannot simply be set up and left alone to achieve their desired results. They require people to support them. People who will ensure these systems are functioning properly and serving their purpose.

When an IT company offers you an hourly support agreement, you can rest assured that the only things that are being supported are those that are making a noise as the proverbial squeaky wheel. Whether your IT support team is internal or outsourced, it is critical to have the right people in the right positions to operate well. It is also critical for these teams to have the depth and capacity to afford them the ability to provide your organization the support that is needed. You simply cannot get that level of support with hourly IT support.

Stuff breaks. It just does. While the hardware and software sectors have improved by leaps and bounds over the years, our tech-based systems are bound to have issues at some point. When they do, having a highly skilled technical support team in your corner can be the difference between a major problem and a minor inconvenience. This team must be able to support both back-end systems, like security and backup solutions, as well as your employees when they run into problems. I will refer to the systems support as the back-end support team, and those who help users as the help desk team. I use the word team because I have rarely run across individuals with the skills to handle both, let alone the capacity. Supporting systems and supporting people are two wildly different worlds.

Most of the highly skilled support engineers who can resolve insanely difficult networking and security issues are the last ones you want to talk to when your email application will not open properly. They may be able to fix the most difficult technical problems, but they are rarely the people you want interfacing with your staff when there is a computer problem. These highly skilled support engineers tend to be overly direct and can leave your users feeling dumb and confused. After all, their gift is 'talking' to computers, not people. The help desk team, on the other hand, needs to understand the problem from the user's perspective and the technical side of the issue. Resolving an issue goes far beyond fixing the technical thing that is broken. While the technical thing may be fixed, the user is having a problem of their own that can cause both fear and frustration; those problems must be resolved as well. It is difficult to hire an individual IT person, either as an employee or a contractor, who can perform well in both worlds. As someone who has hired a great many IT professionals over the years, I can assure you of that. They do exist, and when I find them, they get an offer to join our team; but most IT professionals out there are truly only suited to serve the back-end side or the help desk side - not both. For your organization's technical systems and users to receive the support they need, you must find a team who can handle both.

Back-end Support

The back-end support team is critical to your operations. With so many highly technical systems that require maintenance and management, this team needs to not only understand their innerworkings, but be present and available to identify and rectify problems before they become major issues. If all you have is a help desk team who makes your users happy - but they are not watching over your backup infrastructure - you will be in a world of hurt when your systems crash, and you find out the team can't restore the lost data. Not only do you need a team which can perform this work, they must also be afforded the availability to do it. When your support team lacks the capacity to tackle back-end issues before they become major problems, you will find the back-end issues go by the wayside with little attention paid to them. The squeaky wheel, those immediate problems with computers squeaking for attention, end up getting the grease. It is usually the more subtle noise from a back-end system that is not preventing users from working that ends up being ignored until it is too late. Throughout this book, we have seen the importance of monitoring back-end solutions to ensure they are running properly. However, having these systems monitored and set to provide alerts when trouble is on the horizon is useless if nobody is listening when the systems call out for help.

Help Desk Support

I believe that good help desk support is a beautiful form of art. I am sure you have seen plenty of bad art in your life. If you have not, or you just want a good laugh, feel free to take a few minutes to do a search on Reddit for "delusional artist." Whether you can picture some bad art in your head - or you just lost an hour of your life because I sent you to Reddit - you can draw the connection between the delusional artist on Reddit and the last time you called an 800 number for technical support. Not only did you likely waste a bunch of time on hold listening to terrible elevator music, but you probably ended up with your problem only partially resolved. I will bet the experience left you with an unhealthy dose of frustration. It is all too common to receive bad technical support.

Usually, bad technical support looks like this: someone who is doing everything they can to make you go away rather than solve the problem you are experiencing. Help desk support success is typically measured by metrics that have little to do with user satisfaction or actual resolutions. It is typically measured by the time it takes to close out an issue and the number of issues a support technician can resolve during their shift: quantity not quality. While everyone wants their organization to have all their problems resolved quickly, there is a big difference between what a typical help desk manager and the person who is experiencing the problem will consider to be a "resolution." If you are working with an individual or team who lacks the capacity and drive to go above and beyond, you are destined to continue receiving bad support.

These teams cannot operate independently. While it is ideal if a help desk technician can resolve the issue with the user directly, that is not always the case. Oftentimes there are issues related to the back-end systems that are causing a problem for the user. The most common approach to this is for the issue to be escalated to a higher level of support. As you have likely experienced, the higher up the support ladder you go, the more confused and frustrated you become. I am not sure if this is another tactic to try and get the user to just 'go away' so the issue can be marked as resolved, but it often feels that way. The most effective way I have found to handle issues that require escalation is to keep the highly skilled help desk person involved. But this only works if your help desk is staffed by individuals who are great at working with both people and technology. The help desk tech should be there to guide the user through the resolution process. While the back-end tech may directly interface with the user or their computer, the help desk tech should be there to ensure the user is getting what they need, and to sometimes simply act as a translator.

If you have ever managed this type of team, you may be reading along, thinking to yourself: "This guy is a fool - why on earth would he make people spend that much time with a low-level help desk tech?" The real question you should be asking is why on earth do I have high level help desk technicians spend that much time with basic issues? The answer is simple. I am looking at different metrics than you are. I am not looking at the time it took to close a ticket, or the number of tickets a tech can close in a day. I am looking at how many clients we have who are eager to renew their services with us each year because they are getting what they need.

For your organization to have the back-end support and help desk support you need, your IT team must have depth. Achieving this with an internal IT team is typically extremely difficult or impossible for small- to medium-sized organizations. These people are expensive to hire. Maintaining multiple dedicated individuals within your organization is usually not an option. Organizations which hire these positions internally often end up with one or two overworked employees who lack the ability and capacity to serve these needs. Managing these individuals or small teams can be a huge challenge in and of itself.

By reading this book, you are far better suited than most managers ever will be to hire a capable IT team - but this does not mean that hiring IT professionals in-house is the most effective and cost-efficient use of your time. Therefore, most organizations your size choose to outsource their IT management and I recommend you do too.

CHAPTER SUMMARY

» Having technical support is not the same thing as having IT service. Many organizations find someone to provide tech support and call it a day.

» As we have learned throughout this book, there is much more to IT than fixing technology when it breaks. It is a key component to properly managing your IT though.

» To be successful you must have a team that is capable of supporting both your back-end systems and infrastructure as well as your employees and their computers. It is rare that an individual can excel at both tasks.

» Your support team requires unique skill sets that make them successful in each of these areas. They must work together with a common goal. The team needs to have depth both for knowledge and for availability.

» While it is likely you have outsourced your IT to a Managed Service Provider, you still need to interface with the support team and manage the relationship. Managing these teams can present challenges, but the content of this book should give you an advantage and allow you to speak their language.

Chapter 12:

SELECTING AND VETTING A MANAGED SERVICE PROVIDER

Between financial impacts to your bottom line and the managerial challenges of maintaining an internal IT department, it makes sense for small- and medium-size organizations to outsource their IT to a Managed Service Provider (MSP). There are key differences between outsourcing IT support, hiring someone or a company that you can call when things break, and outsourcing your overall IT management to an MSP. As we explored in the last chapter, simply having outsourced IT support is not enough, and there are many things to consider when vetting and selecting a Managed Service Provider who can truly meet your needs.

In this chapter we will look at the questions that should be asked when vetting a potential service provider – and the answers you should be looking for. Taking the time to read this book is a huge step for your organization; the information in this chapter will afford you a far better chance of finding a vendor who can provide the services you need. By knowing specifically what to ask and what to look for, you will be properly prepared to make a decision that will serve you well into the future.

The first question is not for your potential Managed Service Provider: it's for you. Do you value your data, client data, and employee productivity enough to invest in protecting it? Before searching for an MSP, answer this question within your organization. If you are the only one who values these things but are not the key decision maker, you will have your work cut out for yourself as you seek to persuade the higher-ups. You can start by sharing some of the information in this book. Your management team needs to be on-board to ensure financial commitment and to ensure compliance with new operational procedures that may result from this change. If you can secure a financial commitment from your organization but know that you still have some hesitant individuals on your team, make sure to let the potential MSPs know this. They should tailor their proposal and presentation to your team to help get those last few individuals to buy in.

Now that we have gotten the introspective question out of the way, here are some questions to ask while interviewing MSPs - and the types of answers you should be looking for.

Q: What types of threats are organizations like ours facing that you will help protect us against?

A: The MSP should be able to answer this specifically to your industry, your way of working, and your size. Good answers will go beyond the general cybersecurity threats that are out there; they should also show a firm understanding of current threats. Look for answers that address your physical infrastructure, potential user error, or mistakes and items that address any unique systems you use. Be wary of scare tactics. There is a fine line between being honest about the threats your organization faces and someone using fear alone as a sales tool.

Q: What role will you play in helping us plan for the future, and how involved will you be?

A: They should be able to speak specifically about tasks they will perform, such as budgetary planning and computer replacement cycles. For the MSP to be truly effective in this area, they should propose regular meetings with management - at least a couple of times each year, if not quarterly. They should be able to tell you what those meetings will look like and how they will operate.

Look for the MSP's interest in helping you evolve and develop in your use of technology as well. If the only solutions they offer are ones that stick with the status quo, they might not be involved enough to see potential new solutions that would be beneficial for you. A good MSP should bring these solutions to your attention when they make sense.

Q: Will you interface with our other vendors to make sure all our systems work together?

A: This is a softball question. The MSP should be able to detail what their vendor management process looks like and give examples of how it works with their existing clients. Do not hesitate to ask them if they have a change management process they use. This will give you a good insight into their overall methodology behind introducing solutions into your organization and allow you to see how serious they are about ensuring the work they do avoids negative impacts. You should get a feel for what level of interaction you can expect from them. In an ideal world, they will tell you that all trouble with tech related systems should go to them, and that they will be the ones to engage the vendor if it is not a solution they support. If the MSP is not willing to go to those lengths, it may not be a dealbreaker; however, it is preferable to have a provider who will go to this level to ensure you are taken care of.

Q: What types of problems do you monitor computers for, and what type of maintenance tasks do you perform regularly?

A: Most MSPs will monitor for similar technical issues, so we are not necessarily looking for specific technical answers. Asking this question will give you the opportunity to see how they answer a technical question to a non-technical person. They should give you examples that are easy to understand, in a way that does not make your eyes glaze over as soon as they start talking. If they start talking in 'nerd speak' and show a complete disregard for who their audience is, that is a preview of what your employees will experience when they are looking for technical support. While the person you are talking to may not be the one responding to support requests, the culture of the MSP can be seen via this question. If they are all tech all the time, they may not be a good fit. On the other hand, if they don't seem to understand the tech themselves then you may just be getting a flashy sales pitch.

Q: How do you handle system updates and urgent patches?

A: Like the previous question regarding monitoring and maintenance, the tools used by MSPs are relatively similar across the industry. These tools are well designed and do their job when managed properly. It is highly unlikely that the prospective MSP will offer a revolutionary solution to this problem. You are looking for two things here. First, are they using a specific tool to manage this? There are many IT support firms who want to call themselves an MSP, but who do not actually have the processes in place to carry out the required tasks. If the prospective MSP mentions built-in automatic updates, you can save yourself some time and cut the meeting short. No need to waste any more of your time.

The second and most important thing you are looking for is how serious they are about security. Lots of IT folks love to talk about fancy security solutions, but one of the most important aspects of security is good patch management. The prospective MSP should be able to tell you how frequently they perform updates, and the criteria they use to approve the updates that will be installed. They should also be able to give you some insight into their process for applying urgent updates that are not part of the normal update schedule.

Q: What added layers of security will you provide for our network and computers?

A: Assuming they didn't just tell you that they rely on Microsoft's automatic updates for Windows, and you are still in the meeting, give them the chance to talk about the enhanced security features they offer. While this is an opportunity for the MSP to toss you a lot of trendy marketing speak, it is also an opportunity to see if they are keeping up to date. If they only talk about firewalls and antivirus, you are likely dealing with an MSP that is stuck in the past and is not evolving. Look for terms like 'next gen', 'adaptive' and 'AI'. Sure, some of these terms may be a bit of marketing hype, but you will know if they are using modern solutions and staying on the leading edge of cybersecurity. If you want to go deeper, do not hesitate to ask them to explain some of those terms and how they are beneficial to you.

Q: What type of training will you provide to our team?

A: They should tell you how they will train your team to use some of the solutions they provide, such as a password manager or their remote access solution. This will give you a good idea about how serious they are about you using their solutions. If they do not have a training program in place, then they may not be serious about helping you resolve problems.

At this point in the conversation, the MSP should bring up cybersecurity training for employees. Not only should they tell you that they offer it, but they should be able to explain how their program works. Saying they can provide cybersecurity training without a clear program in place is another sign that the MSP does not take it seriously. They should have a program in place and be able to tell you exactly how it works.

Q: How will your backups work for our systems, what type of testing do you do to ensure backups are working properly, and how frequently do you test them?

A: The solution they provide will depend greatly on how your organization operates. If you have a hefty server infrastructure that you rely on heavily, they should be talking about a full Business Continuity and Disaster Recovery solution. Refer back to Chapter 9 to brush up on this topic. If all your systems are cloud-based, they should be able to tell you about the backup they will provide for those systems. While it is highly unlikely that they will have gotten this far in the conversation only to tell you that, "It's in the cloud, so it doesn't need to be backed up", save yourself a little time and wrap up the meeting now if they do. The MSP should be able to tell you *how* backups are tested and *how frequently* they are tested. Different solutions come with different testing options, so the method is not as important as the fact that they have a testing procedure and a schedule for testing. While you may not care to actually ever see the testing reports, it doesn't hurt to ask the MSP if they would be able to provide them. They may not have a great reporting tool for this, but they should be able to offer you some sort of evidence that these tests are being done.

Q: Do your services include a way for our employees to work remotely?

A: Not all MSPs will offer a remote access solution as part of their services, and this does not need to be a deal breaker. A lot of remote access solutions are dependent on your network and can rely heavily on the hardware you have in place. It is great if they have a solution to offer, but if they do not, the MSP should be able to talk intelligently about a solution they will help you put together. Do not hesitate to ask them to explain what makes their solution secure. Refer back to Chapter 10 for the details the MSP should include, and for methods like opening the firewall for RDP access that should throw up red flags if they are mentioned.

Q: How much support time will be covered by our agreement?

A: It is common for MSPs to offer different tiers of service, with the amount of covered support time being the differentiating factor. They may offer limited remote and onsite support; unlimited remote but limited onsite support; or a completely unlimited support option for both remote and onsite. The lower tiered services may give you some flexibility and allow you to save a little bit of money some months. My recommendation is to at least make sure you have unlimited remote support covered by your agreement. This will allow your team to reach out to the MSP directly for assistance, without you having to keep a watchful eye on the amount of billed support time that has been used in a month. With unlimited remote support, your employees will report issues sooner because they will have direct access to a support team. This can prevent them from dealing with those problems until they become major roadblocks in getting their work done.

Unless your organization operates with a 100% work-from-home structure, ensure that at least some onsite support time is included. Again, this will allow for issues to be resolved before they become a problem, since a tech knows they can proactively come onsite without you incurring a huge bill. Whether the onsite support is included in your agreement or not, ensure the MSP can provide it. If you have people who work in an office and the MSP cannot provide onsite support because they are located outside of your area, you need to look locally. Remote support and management are incredibly powerful, but it is useless if your network is down.

Q: What type of work would not be covered under our support agreement?

A: Look for a clear definition from the MSP regarding what constitutes as support, a project, or professional services. Their agreement may not only cover support; it may also cover a certain amount of project time or professional services time. The MSP's definitions of each should be clear so that you know what is and is not covered. What they define as support should cover troubleshooting software and hardware to resolve problems for both back-end and user facing systems. Most flat-rate support agreements will not cover projects. This is to be expected and should work in your favor financially. 'Projects' include things like replacing a bunch of computers during a refresh cycle or upgrading server or network equipment - these things do not happen on a monthly basis, so you shouldn't need to pay as if they do.

What may fall into the category of 'projects' for some MSPs will be specifically defined as 'professional services' by others and billed at a higher rate. These services typically cover highly technical work that is done to create a solution that is unique to your organization. For example: an MSP creates a custom web portal for your employees to access certain internal resources or designs a highly sophisticated network to allow for specific functionality. Again, these types of services are not performed regularly, so it is in your best interest to only pay for them when you need them. Along with clear definitions of services, have a clear process by which the MSP gains approval prior to providing project or professional services. By defining these services and an approval process, there should then be little to no confusion when it comes to billing from your MSP.

I can assure you that there are several spectacular Managed Service Providers across the world. Our industry sets a high bar. But that is not to say all MSPs are created equal. There are several 'IT companies' who have rebranded as an MSP, but fail to provide the services that are necessary to properly manage your IT. By reading this book, you now understand the core areas within your Information Technology solutions that must be properly managed. You have the tools to not only properly vet a provider, but also to manage your organization's relationship with them moving forward. I encourage you to use this knowledge to implement solutions that will protect your organization and allow for efficiency in your workforce.

You now have the tools. Go put them to use.

CHAPTER SUMMARY

» Most small- to medium-size organizations will outsource their IT management to a Managed Service Provider (MSP).

» Not all MSPs are created equal. When searching for an MSP there are specific things to look for that will allow you to determine how equipped they are to serve your needs.

» Use the provided questions to help identify if they are a good fit for your organization.

» By reading this book and learning about the aspects of your organization's technology and how they are properly managed will allow you to not only find the correct MSP but to effectively work with them to ensure future success.

EPILOGUE

This book was written over the course of 2020 and the beginning of 2021. As I moved from chapter to chapter, the world continued to change. Government entities that were thought to be secure were breached at a massive level. Over 700 Starlink satellites were launched into space as part of Elon Musk's quest to create a high-speed internet service that can be accessed from anywhere in the world. While the world will continue to change, new threats will appear, and technology will continue to advance, the principles within this book hold true. If I had to sum up my message in one statement, it would be this:

Hope is a bad strategy when it comes to IT management and security.

It is my hope that after reading this book, you are no longer relying on hope. You know what to do to keep your data and your people safe.

There are a few topics regarding IT management and security that are important to cover but did not merit their own chapter. Below, you will see some of these. I have included information that will be useful and helpful for your organization, all in the name of helping you protect your IT and your business.

CYBER INSURANCE

With the current state of cyber threats, it is critical for your organization to carry an insurance policy to cover a cyber incident. Your MSP will have their own policy, but it will only cover incidents that happen due to a failure or breach in their systems. If your employee falls for a phishing attack that leads to a breach or financial loss, you need to have insurance in place to help you recover. Some MSPs, like ours, work with insurance providers who are willing to offer you a high-quality plan at a reduced rate based on the services the MSP provides. Talk with your MSP to see if their carrier offers this option. Going through your MSP can be a great way to secure the coverage you need at a better price point. If that is not an option, keep digging. Reach out to your insurance carrier and get a policy in place as soon as possible.

TELEPHONE SERVICES & VOIP

The days of using analog telephone lines are behind us. Sure, there are a lot of these systems still in place, but there are very few of them being deployed anymore. Many MSPs will offer Voice over Internet Protocol (VoIP) phone services. Some do a great job, and others just add it to their services to fill a need without being specifically qualified to support it. If your MSP offers VoIP services, make sure to talk to their other clients who utilize the service; get their feedback before adding it on.

Voice services is one of the things, as of now, that we at Chartered Technology have elected to stay away from. It takes a qualified and experienced team to manage VoIP solutions, and currently, that is not us. If you are not getting this service from your MSP, ensure your MSP and your VoIP phone provider are set up for success. With phones running on your local network and internet service, the MSP and VoIP provider need to be able to work together to troubleshoot problems when they occur. If your voice provider will not work hand-in-hand with your MSP, you are destined for trouble. At Chartered Tech, we have developed a relationship with a local VoIP provider. They are great at what they do, and we can work together when our mutual clients have issues. We trust them and they trust us. Our clients who have other voice providers run into problems more frequently, and the resolution times are longer. VoIP providers are notorious for pointing the finger at your local network and telling you that the issue is your problem, not theirs. Without a good relationship between your VoIP provider and your MSP, there may be more time spent pointing fingers than resolving your issue.

IOT DEVICES

As Internet of Things devices such as internet-connected surveillance cameras and smart speakers become more and more popular, you should expect them to show up at work. There is nothing wrong with having a firm policy against these devices being on your network but enforcing it will be an uphill battle. If or when you do allow these devices at work, make sure to work with your MSP to create a network that is dedicated to these types of devices. That network should be isolated from the rest of your systems so they cannot be used as an entry point for malicious activity. Make sure these devices are updated regularly, as we continue to find vulnerabilities in them. While they may be isolated from causing problems to the rest of your network, there is still room for concern about who could get access to the device and watch the live video or listen in on what people in your office are saying.

PRODUCTIVITY MONITORING

On occasion, we get asked by clients if we can monitor the productivity of their employees, especially remote employees. There are many solutions available for providing this monitoring. I caution you, though. While these systems can be helpful and provide valuable data, they can also cause major problems for your organization if the person responsible for them is not using them effectively or fairly. If you elect to deploy a productivity monitor, make sure there are clear policies for the managers who use them. Make sure they are used to provide incentives to employees rather than create a negative atmosphere where your employees feel like they are constantly being watched by Big Brother.

TECH FOR REMOTE WORKERS

If you are going to have a remote workforce, set them up for success by investing in business-grade computers, monitors, printers and peripherals. Problems with cheap, consumer-quality hardware can kill your remote employees' productivity. You may save a few bucks initially but cutting corners will cost you greatly over time.

I could probably write another whole book's worth of "Oh, and don't forget this too" type things, but I'll leave you with these for now. If I can be of assistance to you, please do not hesitate to reach out to me. You can contact me at:

www.speakingtheirlanguage.com/contact

In the words of the great philosopher, Red Green,
"Remember I'm pullin' for ya – we're all in this together"

Rob Protzman

P.S. If you have not gone and gotten the resources I mentioned throughout this book, head over to www.speakingtheirlanguage.com/thekit to get everything in a single download. These are great free resources that I want you to have and to use.

Speaking Their Language | Rob Protzman

ENDNOTES

1   https://www.npr.org/2016/04/17/474525392/attention-students-put-your-laptops-away

2   https://aws.amazon.com/message/41926/

3   https://www.techradar.com/news/90-percent-of-data-breaches-are-caused-by-human-error

4   https://www.cisa.gov/news/2021/01/05/joint-statement-federal-bureau-investigation-fbi-cybersecurity-and-infrastructure

5   https://nakedsecurity.sophos.com/2015/10/28/did-the-fbi-really-say-pay-up-for-ransomware-heres-what-to-do/

6   https://www.fbi.gov/scams-and-safety/common-scams-and-crimes/ransomware

7   https://heimdalsecurity.com/blog/ransomware-payouts-of-2020/

8   https://www.reuters.com/article/us-japan-stocks-president/tokyo-stock-exchange-ceo-resigns-over-system-failure-idUSKBN28A0DF

CPSIA information can be obtained
at www.ICGtesting.com
Printed in the USA
BVHW041555030921
615980BV00019B/1231